Leadership Roles of the Old Testament

Leadership Roles
of the Old Testament

KING, PROPHET, PRIEST, AND SAGE

Marty E. Stevens

 CASCADE *Books* • Eugene, Oregon

LEADERSHIP ROLES OF THE OLD TESTAMENT
King, Prophet, Priest, and Sage

Cascade Books
An Imprint of Wipf and Stock Publishers
199 W. 8th Ave., Suite 3
Eugene, OR 97401

www.wipfandstock.com

ISBN 13: 978-1-61097-408-0

Cataloging-in-Publication data:

Stevens, Marty E., 1953–
    Leadership roles of the Old Testament : king, prophet, priest, and sage / Marty E. Stevens.

    xii + 122 p. ; 21.5 cm. Includes bibliographical references and index.

    ISBN: 978-1-61097-408-0

    1. Leadership in the Bible. 2. Kings and rulers —Biblical teaching. 3. Prophets. 4. Priest, Jewish. I. Title.

BS1199 .L4 S74 2012

Manufactured in the USA

Contents

Acknowledgments

THIS BOOK IS A sequel of sorts to my previous book, *Theological Themes of the Old Testament: Creation, Covenant, Cultus, and Character*, published by Cascade Books in 2010. A fortuitous encounter with editor K. C. Hanson at the Society of Biblical Literature meeting in November 2008 led to that book and now to this one, when K. C. suggested a sequel that would connect leadership roles of the Old Testament with the themes. So, here it is, once again proving the benefits of collaborative conversation with colleagues.

Teaching "Introduction to the Old Testament" to students at Lutheran Theological Seminary at Gettysburg for six years has been a laboratory for honing the highlights of these four leadership roles, and I am indebted to them for teaching me along the way. My friend Timothy E. Braband and my assistant Julie A. Ritter read drafts and provided the helpful perspective of smart people of deep faith. Dean Robin J. Steinke, the faculty, and staff at Gettysburg Seminary continue to provide a place for me to flourish. My mother, Ruby M. Stevens, provides support and encouragement in ways that only a mother can. Thanks to you all.

Preface

THE OLD TESTAMENT IS an ancient collection of theological reflections on life with God that the Church has claimed as authoritative Scripture. Most of us become acquainted with the Old Testament by reading selected passages in worship services, learning certain stories in Sunday School, or reading brief devotional texts. Introductory books and courses on the Old Testament typically march through the canon chronologically from Genesis to Malachi, highlighting key characters and events along the way. This book, however, engages the Old Testament by investigating four primary leadership roles described in the texts.

Two particular texts were instructive in choosing the four leadership roles, each text located in a prophetic book dated from around the time of the Exile to Babylon in 587 BCE. The prophet Ezekiel announces God's intention for judgment: "Disaster comes upon disaster, rumor follows rumor; they shall keep seeking a vision from the *prophet*; instruction shall perish from the *priest*, and *counsel* from the elders. The *king* shall mourn, the prince shall be wrapped in despair, and the hands of the people of the land shall tremble. According to their way I will deal with them; according to their own judgments I will judge them. And they shall know that I am the LORD" (Ezek 7:26–27; my emphasis). The prophet Jeremiah recalls the hostile reaction from his audience: "Then they said, 'Come, let us make plots against Jeremiah—for instruction shall not perish from the *priest*, nor counsel from the *wise*, nor the word from the *prophet*. Come, let us bring charges against him, and let us not heed any of his words"' (Jer 18:18; my emphasis). These texts summarize the leadership of society into four roles: king, prophet, priest, and sage.

By virtue of the leadership roles selected, certain books of the canon will be emphasized more than others. Where appropriate, I have included information about these leadership roles from other cultures, in an effort to illuminate ancient Israel's understanding of the leader. As described in the Acknowledgments, the book is designed specifically to connect with four primary themes of the Old Testament explored in a previous publication. So, while this book on leadership roles can stand on its own, readers will find that material in this book supplements and reinforces material in the previous book.

The first chapter examines the role of the *King* in ancient Israelite society, serving as the earthly regent of the Divine King, who is also the Creator. Duties of the king are explored, as well as the beneficial and detrimental effects of power.

The second chapter addresses the role of the *Prophet*, especially important as a counterbalance to the monarchy. Called and commissioned by God to read the societal context and speak the truth, prophets relentlessly exhorted the king and the nation to be loyal to the covenant God had made with them.

The third leadership role is that of *Priest*, the intermediary with the divine by means of worship rituals of the cultus, divination of the divine will, and teaching the divine law. The chapter explores the gracious ways God provides to become immediately accessible to the chosen people.

The final chapter addresses the leadership role of *Sage*, the wise advisor of king and family. Probably the least familiar role of the four, we examine Old Testament texts across the canon, and especially in the Wisdom literature, to glean how the sage's advice helped to build character in ancient Israel.

The intended audience for this book is lay people who want to know more about the Old Testament, whether in personal study, church groups, college classrooms, or seminary courses.

Accordingly, I have deliberately avoided dense 'academic' language. Footnotes are not provided because the information presented here is either well-known in scholarly circles or the product of my own scholarship. Those interested in further reading on each theme will find suggestions at the end.

The ancient texts are taken seriously enough not to be taken literally. That is, I understand the Old Testament texts to be *theological* texts first and foremost, not texts that Westerners would label as history or science. Further, the literary history of the Old Testament texts is extremely complicated, involving multiple authors and multiple editors over multiple centuries. I distinguish, therefore, between the world of the narrative (that is, what the story wants the reader to think) and the world of the author (that is, the historical or social circumstances of the author). Holding these together in creative tension allows modern readers to step into the ancient texts and learn something about who God is and who we are as servant leaders of the great Leader.

one

KING

THE FIRST LEADERSHIP ROLE explored is the role of king, monarch of a particular territory, who rules over the inhabitants therein. Throughout the ancient Near East, the king as the supreme ruler was the most common form of governance.

Terminology

The common Hebrew word for king is *melek*, occurring almost 3,000 times in the Old Testament. Found in cognate form in virtually every other ancient Semitic language, the word was clearly well-used in the ancient Near East. Less used in Hebrew is the participle form of the verb *mashal*, "to rule," that is, "one who rules" or "ruler."

In the Old Testament, "king" is the generic term to indicate the person in charge of a territory, ranging in size from a small city to a vast empire. For example, King Hiram was the king of Tyre, a small island to the northwest of Israel in what is now Lebanon. Tyre was the leading city of Phoenicia, renowned for its seafaring abilities and capitalizing on its supply of purple dye, greatly desired in the ancient Near East. But Tyre was a small city, with a population under 100,000 inhabitants even in its heyday. At the other extreme, at the height of the Persian empire headed by King Darius, the controlled territory stretched from India to Greece and included probably in excess of 50 million inhabitants. Even though each is called 'king,' there are clear differences in their power. Obviously, King Hiram had much less power and influence than King Darius. For those readers not familiar with ancient geo-political realities, it can be difficult to know what kind of 'king' the Old Testament is describing. The spectrum covered by 'king' encompasses people we would consider 'mayors' to those we would call 'emperors.'

The Role of King in Society

Lots of people are called 'king' in the Old Testament; even two books are named by that title, 1 Kings and 2 Kings, because they describe the reigns of kings in Israel and Judah from the end of David's reign to the Babylonian exile, a period of about 400 years. What may not be as obvious to casual readers of the Old Testament is the assertion that, despite these human kings, God is the true King (with a capital *K*). In this section, we explore God as King and the means of selecting the earthly king.

God as King

Since kingship was the virtually universal method of governance in the ancient Near East, we should not be surprised that people envisioned the deity as King. Just as the king on earth sat on a throne and ruled the territory, so God sat on a throne in heaven and ruled. The psalmist asserts, "The LORD has established his throne in the heavens, and his kingdom rules over all" (Ps 103:19). (The word LORD in all capital letters indicates to the English reader the underlying Hebrew word YHWH, the personal name of the God of Israel.) The prophet known as Third Isaiah records, "Thus says the LORD: Heaven is my throne and the earth is my footstool" (Isa 66:1a). Just as the king on earth was robed in fine garments befitting his elevated status, so God is robed as King: "The LORD is king, he is robed in majesty; the LORD is robed, he is girded with strength" (Ps 93:1a). When the prophet Isaiah describes his vision, he depicts God as King: "In the year that King Uzziah died, I saw the Lord sitting on a throne, high and lofty; and the hem of his robe filled the temple" (Isa 6:1). Just as the king on earth utilized a staff or scepter as a symbol of rule and authority, so God rules with a scepter: "Your throne, O God, endures forever and ever. Your royal scepter is a scepter of equity" (Ps 45:6). That is, God is imagined as King, with all the royal accoutrements that earthly kings have—throne, footstool, robes, and scepter. Earthly kings also have messengers to communicate their instructions to others. In the Bible, angels fulfill the role of God's royal messengers. In fact, the Hebrew word *mala'k* means both messenger and angel. (Even though they look similar, the word for king, *melek*, is from the root "to rule" and the word for messenger, *mala'k*, is from the root "to send.") In Chapter 2, we will explore how the royal messenger formula of the ancient Near East made its way into the speech pattern of the prophets as they explained their sense of being called as God's messengers.

The theology of God as King supports and reinforces God as Creator and Sustainer of the universe. That is, the two roles of God as Creator and God as King go hand in hand. God created all things and God rules over all things. Consider the following words of the ancient psalmist: "For the LORD is a great God, and a great King above all gods. In his hand are the depths of the earth; the heights of the mountains are his also. The sea is his, for he made it, and the dry land, which his hands have formed" (Ps 95:1–3). First, we note that God is King "above all gods." That is, the texts in the Old Testament frequently witness to the reality of other deities; the point is that for Israel, God is the only legitimate deity to be worshiped and obeyed. Other nations may worship and obey other deities, but Israel is to worship and obey this God known as LORD because this God is the King over all the other gods.

Second, the psalmist explicitly connects God's authority as King over all the world with God's role as Creator of all, using a literary device known as a merism. By naming opposites— depths and heights, sea and land—the psalmist means to include everything in between as created by God and, therefore, subject to God's rule as King. Not only is God ruling as King over all the other gods, God is ruling as King over the created universe, including all of nature and all creatures who inhabit the depths, heights, sea, and land. Above we noted the psalmist's acclamation, "The LORD is king, he is robed in majesty; the LORD is robed, he is girded with strength" (Ps 93:1a). The second half of the verse explicitly connects kingship and creation: "He has established the world; it shall never be moved" (Ps 93:1b). Consider the opening verses of Psalm 104:

> Bless the LORD, O my soul.
> O LORD my God, you are very great.
> You are clothed with honor and majesty,
> wrapped in light as with a garment.
> You stretch out the heavens like a tent,
> you set the beams of your chambers on the waters,
> you make the clouds your chariot,
> you ride on the wings of the wind,
> you make the winds your messengers,
> fire and flame your ministers." (Ps 104:1–4)

The psalmist's praise is primarily directed to God as Creator, envisioned as the great cosmic architect and builder. But note the royal imagery also: God is clothed [in royal robes] of honor, majesty, and light; God rides the [royal] chariot of clouds and wind; God sends [royal] messengers of wind, fire, and flame. Although explicit language of kingship is not present, the psalmist depicts God as King.

The Old Testament writers then take the next logical step: Since God is King over other gods and God is King over all Creation, then God is King over all nations of the world. Of course, the nations of the world would not necessarily agree with this assertion, since they would be making similar statements about their own gods. For example, for the Babylonians, Marduk is the King of the whole world. But the witness of the Old Testament is that the God of Israel is the King of all. For example, "Who would not fear you, O King of the nations? For that is your due" (Jer 10:7); "For dominion belongs to the LORD, and he rules over the nations" (Ps 22:28); "God is king over the nations; God sits on his holy throne" (Ps 47:8).

Several implications arise from the assertion that God is King over all nations. First, God as King over all nations can use those nations to bring about God's will on earth. Depending on Israel's submission to God's kingship and participation in God's will, the use of other nations can be good news or bad news. In the eighth century BCE, the prophet Amos announces to the northern kingdom that God would no longer tolerate rampant economic injustice, with the poor exploited and oppressed to increase the riches for the elite wealthy: "Indeed, I am raising up against you a nation, O house of Israel, says the LORD, the God of hosts, and they shall oppress you from Lebo-hamath to the Wadi Arabah [an area from northern Syria to south of the Dead Sea]" (Amos 6:14). A century later, after the conquest of the northern kingdom by Assyria, the prophet Jeremiah describes a similar fate for the southern kingdom of Judah: "The word of the LORD came to me a second time, saying, 'What do you see?' And I said, 'I see a boiling pot, tilted away from the north.' Then the LORD said to me: Out of the north disaster shall break out on all the inhabitants of the land. For now I am calling all the tribes of the kingdoms of the north, says the LORD; and they shall come and all of them shall set their thrones at the entrance of the gates of Jerusalem, against all its surrounding walls and against all the cities of Judah" (Jer 1:13–15). Later in his prophecy, Jeremiah reiterates God's determination to punish Judah: "Therefore thus says the LORD of hosts: Because you have not obeyed my words, I am going to send for all the tribes of the north, says the LORD, even for King Nebuchadrezzar of Babylon, my servant, and I will bring them against this land and its inhabitants, and against all these nations around; I will utterly destroy them, and make them an object of horror and of hissing, and an everlasting disgrace" (Jer 25:8–9). Surely the ancient audience would have gasped to hear the military general turned king of Babylon called "my servant" by the God of Israel. As King over all nations, God can use them as punishing agents against Israel and Judah when necessary.

On the other hand, when Israel and Judah are in trouble, God can use other nations to rescue them. The prophet known as Second Isaiah reassures the exiles in Babylon by referring to God's capacity to use other nations to rescue them. For example, "I stirred up one from the north, and he has come, from the rising of the sun he was summoned by name. He shall trample on rulers as on mortar, as the potter treads clay" (Isa 41:25). The reference to "one from the north" is presumably King Cyrus, the first Persian ruler who conquered Babylon and repatriated the exiles. Second Isaiah specifically names Cyrus as God's instrument of redemption in chapters 44 and 45, quoted extensively here:

> Thus says the LORD, your Redeemer, who formed you in the womb: I am the LORD, who made all things, who alone stretched out the heavens, who by myself spread out the earth; . . . who says of Jerusalem, "It shall be inhabited," and of the cities of Judah, "They shall be rebuilt, and I will raise up their ruins"; who says to the deep, "Be dry—I will dry up your rivers"; who says of Cyrus, "He is my shepherd, and he shall carry out all my purpose"; and who says of Jerusalem, "It shall be rebuilt," and of the temple, "Your foundation shall be laid." Thus says the LORD to his anointed, to Cyrus, whose right hand I have grasped to subdue nations before him and strip kings of their robes, to open doors before him—and the gates shall not be closed: I will go before you and level the mountains, . . . For the sake of my servant Jacob, and

Israel my chosen, I call you by your name, I surname you,
though you do not know me. (Isa 44:24, 26b—45:2a, 4)

There are several remarkable things about this passage. Note
the complex interweaving of political language and creation language, reinforcing the interconnection between God as King and
God as Creator. God can cause a foreign king to rebuild Jerusalem
and God can dry up rivers; God can manage a Persian king by
grasping his hand and God can level mountains. Similar to Psalm
104 mentioned above, even though explicit language of kingship
is absent, allusions to royal rule infuse the text. Cyrus is said to
be called 'shepherd,' a common word used in the Old Testament
to mean 'king.' The acts of rebuilding Jerusalem and laying the
foundation of the temple are royal responsibilities (see below).
Conquering other kings bring royal status and honor. Grasping
by the hand may refer to a ritual of royal acclamation; likewise,
surnaming may reflect the widespread practice of assuming a
throne name upon accession. Most remarkable is that Cyrus is
called the Lord's 'anointed' or Messiah. Cyrus is the only foreign
person in the entire Bible to carry the title Messiah. By the time
of this text, approximately the mid-sixth century BCE, Messiah
was a title associated with a king who would enact God's rule
on earth, ensuring a dominion characterized by peace, justice,
and righteousness. Here, Isaiah claims that God has selected the
Persian King Cyrus as the royal instrument for bringing about
God's Kingdom.

Second, God as King over all nations implies that things are
not always as they seem to be. God is in charge of Israel's fate
despite apparent evidence to the contrary. In the ancient world,
when one nation defeated another, the routine explanation was
that the conquering nation's god was more powerful than the
defeated nation's god. The deity was responsible for protecting
the nation; if the nation was defeated by another, then obviously
the loser's deity was weaker than the victor's deity. Imagine how
difficult it would be to maintain your belief in your nation's god

if your nation was repeatedly conquered and ruled by other nations. This is precisely Israel's history. From the eighth century BCE until the second century BCE, Israel was subject to the rule of Assyria, Babylonia, Persia, and Greece. Briefly independent under the Hasmoneans, also known as the Maccabees, Israel was then conquered and ruled by the Romans beginning in 63 BCE. Nevertheless, in the face of persistent evidence to the contrary, the ancient Israelites continued to believe that God as King of all nations was the God in control of their destiny. It may look like the Assyrian army, supported by the god Asshur, is more powerful than Israel and Israel's god, but the biblical witness is that the God of Israel was only using Assyria without their knowledge to discipline Israel. It may look like Marduk and the Babylonians are powerful enough to capture Jerusalem and exile the leaders, but to the authors of the Old Testament, the God of Israel was using Babylon as a weapon of punishment. Likewise, it may seem to Cyrus that he conquered Babylon with the help of Marduk and decided to repatriate the Israelites as a political strategy, but to the exiled Judeans, the God of Israel was using Cyrus as an instrument of redemption of God's people.

Third, God as King over all nations implies an eschatological hope that all nations will eventually come to recognize the truth of God's kingship. Behind the protracted struggle for freedom in Egypt lies the contest over the identity of the real King, the God of Israel or the king of Egypt. The first time Moses and Aaron go to Pharaoh, they say, "Thus says the LORD, the God of Israel, 'Let my people go, so that they may celebrate a festival to me in the wilderness.' But Pharaoh said, 'Who is the LORD, that I should heed him and let Israel go? I do not know the LORD, and I will not let Israel go'" (Exod 5:1–2). The series of plagues are enacted so that the Pharaoh and the Egyptians "shall know that I am the LORD" (Exod 7:5, 17; 8:10, 22, etc.). Old Testament prophets long for the day when all peoples of the earth will acknowledge and submit to God's rule: "In days to come the mountain of the LORD's house shall be established as the highest of the mountains, and shall be raised above the hills; all the nations shall stream to it. Many peoples shall come and say, 'Come, let us go up to the mountain of the LORD, to the house of the God of Jacob; that he may teach us his ways and that we may walk in his paths.' For out of Zion shall go forth instruction, and the word of the LORD from Jerusalem" (Isa 2:2–3 // Mic 4:2).

Even as God is King over other gods, King over all Creation, and King over all the nations, even more so is God the King over Israel. Several psalm verses may be cited as evidence: "Let Israel be glad in its Maker; let the children of Zion rejoice in their King" [Zion is another name for Jerusalem] (Ps 149:2); "You are my King and my God; you command victories for Jacob" [Jacob is another name for Israel] (Ps 44:4); "Mighty King, lover of justice, you have established equity; you have executed justice and righteousness in Jacob" (Ps 99:4); "Great is the LORD and greatly to be praised in the city of our God. His holy mountain, beautiful in elevation, is the joy of all the earth, Mount Zion, in the far north, the city of the great King" (Ps 48:1–2); "Your solemn processions are seen, O God, the processions of my God, my King, into the sanctuary" (Ps 68:24). Psalms 93, 95–99 especially celebrate God as King of Israel. For this reason, they are sometimes categorized as 'enthronement psalms.' Excavated tablets describe the annual ritual in Babylon, known as the *akitu* festival, in which a reenactment of divine selection takes place over nine days. Based on these psalms, some scholars have posited an annual festival in Israel akin to the *akitu* festival, in which God was reaffirmed as King. Since Israel was influenced by surrounding cultures, such a festival is not impossible, but no other evidence exists to say definitively that such a festival took place.

After defeating the Midianites, perennial enemies of Israel in the time of tribal confederation, Gideon, the commander of the small military unit, was invited to be king. "Then the Israelites said to Gideon, 'Rule over us, you and your son and your grandson also; for you have delivered us out of the hand of Midian.' Gideon said to them, 'I will not rule over you, and my son will not rule over you; the LORD will rule over you'" (Judg 8:22–23). Later, when Samuel is old, the people of Israel come and say, "'Give us a king to govern us.' Samuel prayed to the LORD, and the LORD said to Samuel, 'Listen to the voice of the people in all that they say to you; for they have not rejected you, but they have rejected me from being king over them'" (1 Sam 8:6b–7).

God Selects the Earthly King

Inasmuch as God created and rules over all things, God delegates royal authority. The first use of the verb "to rule" is in the first chapter of Genesis, what I have called elsewhere a 'creation liturgy' (see *Theological Themes of the Old Testament*, 58). "God made the two great lights—the greater light to rule the day and the lesser light to rule the night—and the stars" (Gen 1:16). Here we may surmise that the rule of God over all of creation is partially delegated to the sun and moon, lights that rule the day and night. God delegates authority to humans to "have dominion" over all living creatures (Gen 1:26, 28), a phrase that must be interpreted first and foremost in light of what it means for God to rule as King. Since God's rule is for the benefit of all creation, humanity's rule must likewise be for the benefit of all creation.

More relevant to the discussion here, God delegates royal authority by appointing human representatives to rule over territories. From as far back as there are written records, kings were the head of the territory. And the virtually universal underpinning of royal governance was the ideology of divine selection. Every king ruled at the selection of the deity—at least that's what the king told the people. The deity's selection of the one who would rule the territory was critically important in legitimizing the king's authority. And frankly, that's what the people wanted to believe. By obeying the divine will, the people were guaranteed prosperity, safety, and long life. Because the deity is ultimately in charge of the territory and its inhabitants, the deity has the right to choose the one who will be the divine representative in charge of the territory and its inhabitants. In other words, the Divine King chooses the earthly king. Conversely stated, the earthly king serves at the pleasure of the Divine King. The divine selection process differed across the territories of the ancient Near East, but the ideology was remarkably similar. Understandably so—the king's rule was undeniably legitimate if the king was selected by the deity. Probably the most bombastic example of divine selection is found in the sixth century BCE Cyrus Cylinder: "[Marduk, the chief deity of Babylon] inspected and checked all the countries, seeking for the upright king of his choice. He took the hand of Cyrus, king of the city of Anshan, and called him by his name, proclaiming him aloud for the kingship over all of everything." While it may sound like exaggerated propaganda—searching the whole world for the one person worthy to rule Babylon—the same ideology is operative in the Old Testament.

Psalm 2 is an exemplar of this ideology. The psalmist imagines the other nations conspiring against the king of Israel. As a result, God (in heaven) rejects their conspiracy by saying, "I have set my king on Zion, my holy hill" (Ps 2:6). The Israelite king publicly affirms the divine selection: "I will tell of the decree of the LORD: He said to me, 'You are my son; today I have begotten you'" (Ps 2:7). Using adoption language common in the ancient Near East, the psalmist legitimates the king's rule using the ideology of divine selection. Similarly, the author of Psalm 89 reminds God of previous promises: "Then you spoke in a vision to your faithful one, and said: 'I have set the crown on one who is mighty, I have exalted one chosen from the people . . . I will make him the firstborn, the highest of the kings of the earth'" (Ps 89:19, 27). Likewise, in Psalm 110 God is affirmed as the power behind the throne: "The LORD says to my lord [the king], 'Sit at my right hand until I make your enemies your footstool.' The LORD sends out from Zion your mighty scepter. Rule in the midst of your foes" (Ps 110:1-2). The English notion of the 'Divine Right of Kings' is not far afield from the theology operative in the ancient

Near East. As the One who created the universe and all that is in it, God authorizes the human king as the deputy ruler on earth. Whereas in ancient Egyptian culture and later Roman culture, earthly kings understood themselves to be somehow divine, Israel never worshiped the earthly king. Worship for reserved for God alone, the true King of Israel.

People Select the Earthly King

In addition to an ideology of divine selection of the earthly king, the king was selected by people. The Old Testament depicts four principal ways in which kings assumed or were accorded authority. First, the people themselves could choose a king by popular consensus. Not surprisingly, past deeds on behalf of the people, usually in battle, encouraged the people to elevate the military leader to king, as illustrated in the request to Gideon mentioned above. David's victories over the pesky Philistines no doubt played a part when, "the people of Judah came, and there [in Hebron] they anointed David king over the house of Judah" (2 Sam 2:4a). Seven years later, "all the elders of Israel came to the king at Hebron; and King David made a covenant with them at Hebron before the LORD, and they anointed David king over Israel" (2 Sam 5:3). Even in Old Testament times, the people's acclamation "Long live the king!" signaled their willingness to be governed by this person (see, for example, 1 Sam 10:24; 2 Sam 16:16; and 2 Kgs 11:12).

Second, as we see in the above example about Gideon, the people call for royal rule by "you and your son and your grandson" (Judg 8:22). That is, the king could be selected by virtue of being genetically descended from the previous king. Although scholars debate the date by which dynastic succession was widely practiced, clearly royal lineage was an important factor in selecting a king. Primogeniture, the automatic preference of the firstborn, sometimes led to familial violence. Ancient records sometimes depict convoluted genealogies in order for a claimant to assert his royal heritage.

Third, the throne could be claimed by force, for example, through a military coup. For example, in the mid-ninth century BCE, a succession of military coups resulted in Omri as ruler of the northern kingdom. The narrative is rated R for violence.

> In the twenty-sixth year of King Asa of Judah [883 BCE], Elah son of Baasha began to reign over Israel in Tirzah; he reigned two years. But his servant Zimri, commander of half his chariots, conspired against him. When he was at Tirzah, drinking himself drunk in the house of Arza, who was in charge of the palace at Tirzah, Zimri came in and struck him down and killed him, in the twenty-seventh year of King Asa of Judah, and succeeded him . . . Now the troops were encamped against Gibbethon, which belonged to the Philistines, and the troops who were encamped heard it said, "Zimri has conspired, and he has killed the king"; therefore all Israel made Omri, the commander of the army, king over Israel that day in the camp. So Omri went up from Gibbethon, and all Israel with him, and they besieged Tirzah. When Zimri saw that the city was taken, he went into the citadel of the king's house; he burned down the king's house over himself with fire, and died . . . But the people who followed Omri overcame the people who followed Tibni son of Ginath; so Tibni died, and Omri became king. (1 Kgs 16:8–10, 15b–18, 22)

In the case of a military coup, divine legitimation is all the more critical. Generally speaking, the one now claiming royal power asserts the divine displeasure at the previous king, with a new regime now instituted by the deity. In the verses omitted above, the narrator explains that Zimri killed Elah "because of all the sins of Baasha and the sins of his son Elah that they committed, and that they caused Israel to commit, provoking the LORD God of Israel to anger with their idols" (1 Kgs 16:13); and Omri killed Zimri because "because of the sins that he committed, doing evil in the sight of the LORD, walking in the way of Jeroboam, and for the sin that he committed, causing Israel to sin" (1 Kgs 16:19). Something like this may also lie behind the narrative of Saul's rejection as king and David's rise to power.

Finally, the king could be imposed on the people by a more powerful empire, creating a "puppet king" or a "client king." So, for example, during the reign of Jehoiachin, Nebuchadnezzar besieged Jerusalem and exiled a small number of elites in 597 BCE. Then "the king of Babylon made Mattaniah, Jehoiachin's uncle, king in his place, and changed his name to Zedekiah" (2 Kgs 24:17). When Zedekiah rebelled, Nebuchadnezzar had him killed and appointed Gedaliah over them (2 Kgs 25:22).

Duties of the King

Ideologically speaking, the earthly king was to administer the territory in keeping with the will of the Divine King. The earthly king serves as a conduit for the blessings of the Divine King on the nation: peace, prosperity, justice, and righteousness. In the petitions of Psalm 72, structured as a prayer for the king, we get a job description for the ideal earthly king.

> Give the king your justice, O God,
>> and your righteousness to a king's son.
> May he judge your people with righteousness,
>> and your poor with justice.
> May the mountains yield prosperity for the people,
>> and the hills, in righteousness.
> May he defend the cause of the poor of the people,
>> give deliverance to the needy,
>> and crush the oppressor.
> May he live while the sun endures,
>> and as long as the moon, throughout all generations.
> May he be like rain that falls on the mown grass,
>> like showers that water the earth.

In his days may righteousness flourish
    and peace abound, until the moon is no more.
May he have dominion from sea to sea,
    and from the River to the ends of the earth.
May his foes bow down before him,
    and his enemies lick the dust.
May the kings of Tarshish and of the isles
    render him tribute,
may the kings of Sheba and Seba
    bring gifts.
May all kings fall down before him,
    all nations give him service.
For he delivers the needy when they call,
    the poor and those who have no helper.
He has pity on the weak and the needy,
    and saves the lives of the needy.
From oppression and violence he redeems their life;
    and precious is their blood in his sight.
Long may he live!
    May gold of Sheba be given to him.
May prayer be made for him continually,
    and blessings invoked for him all day long.
May there be abundance of grain in the land;
    may it wave on the tops of the mountains;
    may its fruit be like Lebanon;
and may people blossom in the cities
    like the grass of the field.
May his name endure forever,
    his fame continue as long as the sun.
May all nations be blessed in him;
    may they pronounce him happy. (Ps 72:1–17)

We may think of the duties of the king in three broad categories, each representing the responsibility of the king to secure something very important to the people.

Securing the Property

Physical security of the land and its boundaries is critically important, especially in Israel. Strategically located as a land bridge between Africa and Asia and between Europe and Asia, the importance of controlling the land was far greater than its small size would indicate. Much more powerful empires to the east, south, and west were perennially interested in controlling the territory of Israel in order to exploit the trade routes and in order to utilize the geography as a buffer against other powerful empires. Every ancient nation needed to be able to muster military forces to protect the borders from invaders. When Israel was living as a loose confederation of tribes, charismatic leaders called "judges" would arise at a time of crisis to raise an army in defense of their territory. As we have already seen, Gideon commanded a small band of men who defeated the Midianites (Judges 6–8); similarly, Deborah and Barak defeated the Canaanites (Judges 4–5). By the time of Samuel, the last judge of Israel, the Philistine threat from the southwest seacoast overwhelmed the Israelite tribes settled in the hill country. The last straw may have been the capture of the Ark of the Covenant by the Philistines; if the portable throne of God was taken into captivity by the enemy, what possible chance did Israel have of defeating them? As the story is told, the Philistines experienced all kinds of troubles immediately after capturing the ark and voluntarily returned it (1 Samuel 4–6). At any rate, the elders of Israel come to Samuel and ask, "Appoint for us, then, a king to govern us, like other nations" (1 Sam 8:5b).

The irony, not lost on the astute reader, is that from the time of Israel's election as God's chosen people, their vocation was to be *distinct* from other nations. Yet here they specifically ask for a king so they can be *like* other nations. In asking for a king like all the other nations had, Israel has effectively discounted God's rule as their King. They are saying, in so many words, "God our King is not doing a good enough job defending our property, so we need another king." No wonder God says to Samuel, "Listen to the voice of the people in all that they say to you; for they have not rejected you, but they have rejected me from being king over them" (1 Sam 8:7). Samuel warns the people about the underside of kingship.

> These will be the ways of the king who will reign over you: he will take your sons and appoint them to his chariots and to be his horsemen, and to run before his chariots; and he will appoint for himself commanders of thousands and commanders of fifties, and some to plow his ground and to reap his harvest, and to make his implements of war and the equipment of his chariots. He will take your daughters to be perfumers and cooks and bakers. He will take the best of your fields and vineyards and olive orchards and give them to his courtiers. He will take one-tenth of your grain and of your vineyards and give it to his officers and his courtiers. He will take your male and female slaves, and the best of your cattle and donkeys, and put them to his work. He will take one-tenth of your flocks, and you shall be his slaves. And in that day you will cry out because of your king, whom you have chosen for yourselves; but the LORD will not answer you in that day. (1 Sam 8:11–18)

In essence, Samuel says, "Be careful what you wish for." But the people respond, "No! but we are determined to have a king over us, so that we also may be like other nations, and that our king may govern us and go out before us and fight our battles" (1 Sam 8:19b–20). At the beginning of this episode, the people claimed to want Samuel to appoint them a king because his own sons were unjust. But now it is clear that the need for a standing army is the driving force behind their request. The Philistine threat is so ominous that the people seem willing to accept compulsory military service for their sons, compulsory service in the royal household for their daughters, and financing of the military-industrial complex through taxation and appropriation of property. Security and foreign tranquility seem to be worth any price.

Domestic tranquility is also a part of the king's duty of securing the property. For a king, securing the 'internal boundaries' can be as important as securing the external boundaries. In this vein, kings in the ancient world were depicted as law-givers and guardians of justice. Inasmuch as the earthly king represented the Divine King, the law promulgated by the king originates and reflects the Divine Law. For example, the well-known Code of Hammurabi, carved on a piece of rock over seven feet high, depicts King Hammurabi sitting on his throne and receiving the laws from the chief deities of ancient Babylon about 1750 BCE. In the opening paragraph, the king announces that the gods have chosen him to enact the rule of righteousness and to protect the weak from the strong. In the biblical narrative, Moses receives the Law at Mount Sinai directly from God; the text specifically says, "When God finished speaking with Moses on Mount Sinai, he gave him the two tablets of the covenant, tablets of stone, written with the finger of God" (Exod 31:18). There can be no mistake in the mind of the hearers that the Law in effect for Israel is the Law of the Divine King. The fact that Moses is never understood to be an earthly king only adds to the ideology of God as the only, true King. In Psalm 72, quoted extensively above, the initial petition is for God to grant righteousness and justice to the earthly king as defining characteristics of his reign. Three central verses commend the king for protecting the weak of society from exploitation and oppression (vv. 12–14). In the 'last words' attributed to David, he acknowledges the efficacy of ruling with justice derived from God: "The God of Israel has spoken, the Rock of Israel has said to me: One who rules over people justly, ruling in the fear of God, is like the light of morning, like the sun rising on a cloudless morning, gleaming from the rain on the grassy land" (2 Sam 23:3–4).

Biblical texts seem to indicate judicial cases routinely decided by the elders at the city gates, the ancient equivalent of the county courthouse. The king (or his deputies) may have acted as a court of appeal. As part of Absalom's attempt to seize the throne occupied by his father David, Absalom stationed himself in the city gates of Jerusalem to hear legal claims from persons who came to press claims resolved unsatisfactorily in their own tribal cities. "Absalom would say, 'See, your claims are good and right; but there is no one deputed by the king to hear you.' Absalom said moreover, 'If only I were judge [ruler] in the land! Then all who had a suit or cause might come to me, and I would give them justice.' . . . Thus Absalom did to every Israelite who came to the king for judgment; so Absalom stole the hearts of the people of Israel" (2 Sam 15:3–4, 6). Here, the power of the king to grant justice is used by a royal claimant to garner support for his candidacy. King David's army would later fight the armed forces attached to Absalom, resulting in Absalom's unusual death caused from hanging by his hair caught in a tree (2 Samuel 18). Recall the endearing story of the two women appearing before King Solomon, each claiming to be the mother of the same child (1 Kgs 3:16–28). The final editorial summary is, "All Israel heard of the judgment that the king had rendered; and they stood in awe of the king, because they perceived that the wisdom of God was in him, to execute justice" (1 Kgs 3:28). A direct link is made between the wisdom of God dwelling in the king and justice executed for the people.

Securing the Progeny

At some point in the history of the ancient Near East, the dynastic rule of kings became the normative method of royal succession. As mentioned earlier, the automatic succession of the oldest son is a later development, with the result that sibling rivalry for the throne was rampant. In the southern kingdom of Judah, the dynasty initiated by David ruled almost without interruption for over four hundred years, until the defeat of the monarchy by the Babylonians. The only brief interruption noted in the biblical texts is the seizure of the throne by Athaliah in 842 BCE. A daughter of the ruling family of the northern kingdom, she had been given in marriage to King Jehoram of Judah. When their son, King Ahaziah of Judah, was killed by a military commander who also seized the throne of the northern kingdom from Athaliah's brother, "she set about to destroy all the royal family" (2 Kgs 11:1b). Fearing for the life of Ahaziah's son, a member of the royal family "stole him away from among the king's children who were about to be killed; she put him and his nurse in a bedroom. Thus she hid him from Athaliah, so that he was not killed; he remained with her six years, hidden in the house of the LORD, while Athaliah reigned over the land" (2 Kgs 11:2–3). The child was acclaimed king by the priests and people, at which time Athaliah was executed.

By contrast, in the northern kingdom of Israel, the principle of dynastic succession was not nearly so well established. The first king of the northern kingdom was an army commander acclaimed as king after the ten northern tribes seceded from the reign of Solomon's son. He and his son ruled for twenty-two years, at which time a military coup seized the throne for twenty-four years, until another military coup was successful, and so on. In the two-hundred-year-long life of the northern kingdom, we may count nine different dynasties attempting to be established. The longest was the Omride dynasty, enjoying a reign of about thirty-five years; the shortest can be counted in months. Obviously, fathering sons was an essential ingredient in establishing a royal dynasty. The harder task was to keep them safe from those who would be king.

Securing progeny requires maintaining a royal household: wives, children, and servants need to be housed, fed, clothed, and entertained. No less than today, this was an expensive undertaking in the ancient world. Solomon, just to take one notable example, was engaged with the building of his offices, his own residence, and the residence for his harem for thirteen years (1 Kgs 7:1). "Among his wives were seven hundred princesses and three hundred concubines" (1 Kgs 11:3a). He divided the territory into twelve administrative districts, each of which provided food for the royal household for one month per year (1 Kgs 4:7). "Solomon's provision for one day was thirty *cors* of choice flour, and sixty *cors* of meal, ten fat oxen, and twenty pasture-fed cattle, one hundred sheep, besides deer, gazelles, roebucks, and fatted fowl" (1 Kgs 4:22–23). (A *cor* is about 6.5 bushels; at average consumption rates, the *cors* of flour and meal mentioned could feed over 36,000 people per day.) The author adds, "Solomon also had forty thousand stalls of horses for his chariots, and twelve thousand horsemen . . . They also brought to the required place barley and straw for the horses and swift steeds, each according to his charge" (1 Kgs 4:26, 28). When the Queen of Sheba visits King Solomon, arriving in Jerusalem "with a very great retinue, with camels bearing spices, and very much gold, and precious stones" (1 Kgs 10:2), she quickly realizes that her wealth does not hold a candle to that of Solomon. "When the queen of Sheba had observed all the wisdom of Solomon, the house that he had built, the food of his table, the seating of his officials, and the attendance of his servants, their clothing, his valets, and his burnt offerings that he offered at the house of the LORD, there was no more spirit in her" (1 Kgs 10:4–5). The author summarizes, "The weight of gold that came to Solomon in one year was six hundred sixty-six talents of gold, besides that which came from the traders and from the business of the merchants" (1 Kgs 10:14–15a). Even with exaggeration by the authors to enhance the status of King Solomon, sustaining the royal household was very expensive for the people of the land.

Securing the Presence of the Divine

The third broad category of royal responsibility was to secure the presence and blessing of the deity. For kings across the ancient Near East, the primary way of accomplishing such a goal was to build temples and provide for religious rituals. The common mud-brick temples of Mesopotamia required regular repair. Even if a shrine was structurally sound, kings often renovated them or constructed additions. Excavated texts routinely show kings boasting of their generosity in constructing grandiose temples, authorizing priests to serve at those temples, and contributing funds or commodities to carry out appropriate rites. The annual re-enthronement of the king was often an opportunity for largesse towards temples: donations of people to work at the temples, contributions of commodities for offerings, donations of specialized religious vessels or precious metals to make them, and grants of tax exemptions for a specified period. Lest we think the kings of the ancient Near East acted solely out of altruistic motives, we should remember that the king rules at the pleasure of the Divine King, the deity(ies) worshiped at the temple(s). And the priests are charged with the discernment of the divine will (see further in Chapter 3). So if the king is generous to the priests, perhaps the king can expect a favorable interpretation of the will of the Divine King. Also, even as the king regularly gave to the temples, the king regularly took from the temples, whether 'authorized' withdrawals or not. (See my book *Temples, Tithes, and Taxes: The Temple and the Economic Life of Ancient Israel* for more.)

In the biblical narrative, once King David has secured the property and the progeny, he turns his attention to securing the presence of the divine by building a temple for God in Jerusalem. Until this point, the presence of God has been localized in the Ark of the Covenant, a portable box carried on poles and housed in a tent shrine. David decides to build a permanent 'house' for God. But it was not to be. One version of the story recounts that God makes known through the prophet Nathan that such a permanent 'house' is not necessary; rather, God will build a 'house' for David, that is, a royal dynasty. One of the future members of that dynasty will build a 'house' for God. Even though the divine announcement does not specify which son will succeed David and construct the temple, Solomon emerges as the victorious claimant of the throne and undertakes the building project that results in the first Jerusalem temple.

According to the biblical narrative, Solomon spares no expense in constructing a temple made of dressed stone, paneled with cedars from Lebanon and cypress wood, every surface carved with likenesses of local flora, and every surface covered in gold leaf. Solomon also paid for expert bronze-workers to make the temple accoutrements (lampstands, lavers, pillars, pots, shovels, basins): "Solomon left all the vessels unweighed, because there were so many of them; the weight of the bronze was not determined" (1 Kgs 7:47). Gold was donated by Solomon to make the necessary implements: "the golden altar, the golden table for the bread of the Presence, the lampstands of pure gold, five on the south side and five on the north, in front of the inner sanctuary; the flowers, the lamps, and the tongs, of gold; the cups, snuffers, basins, dishes for incense, and firepans, of pure gold; the sockets for the doors of the innermost part of the house, the most holy place, and for the doors of the nave of the temple, of gold" (1 Kgs 7:48b–50). At its dedication, Solomon provided 22,000 oxen and 120,000 sheep for sacrifice (1 Kgs 8:63). The biblical authors use exaggeration to emphasize the fulfillment of the royal duty of securing the divine presence by the king.

Another version of the story indicates that King David was disqualified from building the temple for God because he had engaged in warfare. "But the word of the LORD came to me, saying, 'You have shed much blood and have waged great wars; you shall not build a house to my name, because you have shed so much blood in my sight on the earth'" (1 Chr 22:8). The text goes on to announce that David's son Solomon, a man of peace, will build the temple. Probably, the text serves to explain first of all, why Solomon and not David built the temple and, secondly, connects the name Solomon [Hebrew *Shlomo*] with the similar sounding Hebrew word for peace, *shalom*. Even though David does not build the temple, according to the Chronicler he makes all the preparations, including the construction materials, the blueprints, and the organization of priests and musicians.

King Hezekiah of Judah is remembered in the biblical texts as a good king second only to King Josiah. The story of his great Passover festival at the end of the eighth century BCE serves as evidence of his attention to the responsibility of the king to secure the divine presence. "For King Hezekiah of Judah gave the assembly a thousand bulls and seven thousand sheep for offerings, and the officials gave the assembly a thousand bulls and ten thousand sheep. The priests sanctified themselves in great numbers . . . There was great joy in Jerusalem, for since the time of Solomon son of King David of Israel there had been nothing like this in Jerusalem" (2 Chr 30:24, 26). A similar phrase is used by a different source at the end of the Passover festival initiated by King Josiah almost a century later: "No such passover had been kept since the days of the judges who judged Israel, or during all the days of the kings of Israel or of the kings of Judah; but in the eighteenth year of King Josiah this passover was kept to the LORD in Jerusalem" (2 Kgs 23:22–23). King Josiah is also remembered in the narrative as refurbishing the Jerusalem temple, at which time the Book of the Law was discovered, initiating nationwide religious reforms.

In addition to temple construction, obedience to the divine will was critical to securing the presence of the deity. In several texts of the Old Testament, the dynastic covenant with David is contingent upon moral behavior. For example, "Now the word of the LORD came to Solomon, 'Concerning this house that you are building, if you will walk in my statutes, obey my ordinances, and keep all my commandments by walking in them, then I will establish my promise with you, which I made to your father David'" (1 Kgs 6:11–12); "Therefore the LORD said to Solomon, 'Since this has been your mind and you have not kept my covenant and my statutes that I have commanded you, I will surely tear the kingdom from you and give it to your servant'" (1 Kgs 11:11); "The LORD swore to David a sure oath from which he will not turn back: 'One of the sons of your body I will set on your throne. If your sons keep my covenant and my decrees that I shall teach them, their sons also, forevermore, shall sit on your throne'" (Ps 132:11–12); "Because King Manasseh of Judah has committed these abominations, has done things more wicked than all that the Amorites [Canaanites] did, who were before him, and has caused Judah also to sin with his idols; . . . I will cast off the remnant of my heritage, and give them into the hand of their enemies; they shall become a prey and a spoil to all their enemies" (2 Kgs 21:11, 14). Even though the ideology of the writers is evident in these texts, to blame King Manasseh for the exile, for example, the linkage between obedience to the divine will and securing the divine presence is paramount.

Limits on the Powers of the King

Not unlike modern rulers, the ancient kings sometimes took advantage of their privileged position as the agent of the Divine King to enrich themselves and their supporters. Taxation, for example, is a mechanism for redistribution of wealth in support of the general good—at least in principle. The populace remits taxes to the governmental authority in return for national defense, social welfare for the weak and needy, maintenance of the government, and so forth. But as we have seen in Samuel's warning cited above, he describes the exploitation that routinely accompanies kingship: conscription of sons and daughters to the royal court, exaction of agricultural and animal products, and appropriation of productive resources. The description of Solomon's needs for the royal household demonstrates the large proportion of taxes going to support the 'lifestyle of the rich and famous.' In ancient Israel, the power of the king was limited in three important ways.

First, the laws of the nation served to limit the king's inclination toward self-enrichment. As noted above, the king promulgated the laws in the ancient world. A noticeable feature of the Code of Hammurabi is that the population is divided into segments for the administration of the laws. The part of the population with the most favorable legal treatment is the upper crust of society, including the royal court, the royal retainers, and professional people. Not surprisingly, slaves had the least favorable treatment in the laws. The checks and balances present in a democratic system of government were not present in ancient monarchies. Since the king made the laws, the king could make laws favorable to himself and his cronies. In ancient Israel, however, the earthly king is specifically noted as being subject to the same laws as everyone else.

> When [the king] has taken the throne of his kingdom, he shall have a copy of this law written for him in the presence of the levitical priests. It shall remain with him and he shall read in it all the days of his life, so that he may learn to fear the LORD his God, diligently observing all the words of this law and these statutes, neither exalting himself above other members of the community nor turning aside from the commandment, either to the right or to the left, so that he and his descendants may reign long over his kingdom in Israel. (Deut 17:18–20)

This, of course, is the idealized version of Israelite kingship that reflects the Kingship of God. Immediately before the admonition for the king to be aware of and subject to the Law, the author explicitly says, the king "must not acquire many horses for himself . . . And he must not acquire many wives for himself, or else his heart will turn away; also silver and gold he must not acquire in great quantity for himself" (Deut 17:16a, 17). We may reasonably expect that the lived experience of kingship in ancient Israel involved many horses, many wives, much silver and gold—and the exploitation that made such wealth possible. The compilers of the Old Testament, however, could at least imagine a situation in which the king humbled himself to the authority of the Law, just like everyone else.

Second, the powers of the monarchy were limited by the military. We saw above how, especially in the northern kingdom, kings were overthrown by military commanders. Control over numbers of armed men certainly made the military commanders a perennial threat to the king. Not surprisingly, the king curried favor with the military by enriching them with wealth and granting favors. A common arrangement in the ancient Near East involved a grant of land by the king to private citizens in return for specified military service. In excavated Mesopotamian texts, the land is labeled according to the type of service the new landowner is expected to render: 'bow-land' for archers, 'horse-land' for cavalry, and 'chariot-land' for charioteers. Unlike today, the soldiers had to outfit themselves for military service with horses, shields, bows and arrows, and so forth. Some texts indicate that they may have also been charged with supplying their own food. For example, "Jesse said to his son David, 'Take for your brothers an ephah [3/4 of a bushel] of this parched grain and these ten loaves, and carry them quickly to the camp to your brothers'" who were engaged in fighting the Philistines (1 Sam 17:17). At the end of a military campaign, the warriors were entitled to share in the booty captured from the defeated enemy. So, for example, "[Joshua] said to them, 'Go back to your tents with much wealth, and with very much livestock, with silver, gold, bronze, and iron, and with a great quantity of clothing; divide the spoil of your enemies with your kindred'" (Josh 22:8). In some battles, however, God specifically eliminates the possibility of booty by commanding the complete destruction of the enemy—people, houses, and livestock (see, for example, Josh 6:16–21). While this extreme violence is offensive, some scholars maintain that the practice of the enemy being 'devoted to destruction' actually *prevented* violence. By denying the warriors any share in the wealth of the enemy (either in the form of people or animals), a significant motivation for violent confrontation is eliminated. Rather, the wealth of the enemy is acquired through treaty negotiations backed by the threat of violence.

Third, alongside the rise of the monarchy in the ancient Near East, we find the rise of the phenomenon known as prophecy. The prophets in the Old Testament are often associated with the royal court, being consulted regularly by kings for directions from God. Some of the prophets seem to be no more than 'yes-men' to the king, telling him what he wants to hear. But most of the prophets speak truth to the power of the monarchy, calling the kings to account for their greed and exploitation of the populace. We will examine the role of prophets in the Old Testament in the next chapter.

The Messiah and the Kingdom of God

The phrase "kingdom of God" does not appear in the Old Testament, although its roots are nourished and grown there. We have seen the widespread conviction that God is the Divine King, whose reign is characterized by justice for all and the wholeness of all creation. The Divine King intends for all creation to flourish to its fullest potential, characterized by abundance and generosity. The Old Testament vision is for such a Divine Reign, that is, the Kingdom of God. And the Old Testament speaks truthfully to the lack of such a vision in real life. For most of the Old Testament narrative, the reigns of the earthly kings do not mirror the reign of the Divine King. Creation does not flourish to its fullest potential. All people of society do not experience justice. Life is not abundant nor generous. In the face of lived reality, the ideal vision of the Divine Reign is pushed into the future. The thought goes, "We may not be experiencing justice and wholeness under this particular king as we should be, but one day a king will arise to govern us who will mirror the Divine Reign." For virtually all of the Old Testament, future history would reveal this righteous king. That is, even though the vision is pushed into the future, it was a future that would take place *in the course of real history.* Said another way, the expectation of the Divine Reign enacted through the earthly king was anticipated for the people in the land of Judah/Israel. The Divine Reign was not understood to be delayed until after death; rather, the Divine Reign brings about the fullness of life in the here and now.

The English word 'Messiah' is a transliteration of the Hebrew noun *meshiach*. The Hebrew noun is derived from the verbal root *mashach* that means "to smear with oil." The Greeks chose the noun *Christos*, because it too is derived from the verb that means "to anoint with oil." The texts that make up the Old Testament understand anointing with oil as a ritual that set apart an object or a person for service, often with religious implications. For example, when Jacob awakens from a dream in which he experiences the presence of God, he erects a stone pillar and pours oil over it (Gen 28:18). In a strict sense, the stone pillar is now a 'messiah'—something smeared with oil and set apart. The recipe for the anointing oil is delivered by the Lord to Moses: "Take the finest spices: of liquid myrrh five hundred shekels [of weight], and of sweet-smelling cinnamon half as much, that is, two hundred fifty, and two hundred fifty of aromatic cane, and five hundred of cassia—measured by the sanctuary shekel [weight]—and a hin [a gallon] of olive oil; and you shall make of these a sacred anointing oil blended as by the perfumer; it shall be a holy anointing oil" (Exod 30:23–25). The oil should be used to smear the tent, the Ark of the Covenant, the table, the lampstand, the altar, and all the utensils (Exod 30:26–29). Again, strictly speaking, all of these items are 'messiahs.'

Most frequently, people are smeared with oil to be set apart for particular service as priests, prophets, and kings. Aaron and his sons are anointed with oil to be set apart for priestly service, first in the Wilderness Tabernacle and then in the Jerusalem temple (Exod 30:30). The practice of anointing prophets and kings may be seen in the divine instructions given to Elijah as he cowered in a cave, fearful of the wrath of Queen Jezebel. God reassures him of his safety and commands, "Go, return on your way to the wilderness of Damascus; when you arrive, you shall anoint Hazael as king over Aram [Syria]. Also you shall anoint Jehu son of Nimshi as king over Israel; and you shall anoint Elisha son of Shaphat of Abel-meholah as prophet in your place" (1 Kgs 19:15). David is anointed king when Samuel pours oil from his ram's horn onto David's head (1 Sam 16:13). The longevity of the Davidic dynasty in the southern kingdom means that the Old Testament frequently uses the phrase 'the Lord's anointed' as a kind of shorthand for 'a king in the dynasty of David.' People smeared with oil and set apart for service as priests, prophets, or kings were 'messiahs.'

The careful reader will have noted that all of the uses of the word 'messiah' to this point have used the lower-case *m*. The Old Testament does not give witness to what is generally meant by Messiah (with a capital *M*). Readers are generally surprised to note that the Old Testament passages typically labeled as "Messianic prophecies" do not even use the word 'messiah.' Isaiah 9:1–7, for example, describes an ideal ruler who will establish justice and righteousness, but nowhere is there any indication of 'messiah' or even anointing. Likewise, Isa 11:1–12 depicts one in the line of David who will enact justice and righteousness, facilitating a peaceable kingdom, but one looks in vain for the word 'messiah' or 'anoint.' Despite the lack of 'messiah' vocabulary, the passages paint a picture of the rule of the Divine King, which would be brought about by the designated earthly king, a 'messiah.' Even in the days of the New Testament, many persons claimed to be messiahs, by which they meant that they were set apart for service that would demonstrate the reign of the Divine King. The theological trajectory that leads to Jesus of Nazareth as the Messiah (with a capital *M*) will take place in the early Church, along with the acclamation of Jesus as 'King of Kings.'

two

PROPHET

THE LEADERSHIP ROLE OF prophet is intimately connected with
the leadership role of the king in the ancient world. In this chapter, we explore the prophetic vocation and message.

Terminology

The English word 'prophet' comes from the Greek word *prophetes*,
the combination of the preposition *pro*, "before," and the verbal
root *phe-*, "to speak." The noun is what is often called an "agent
noun," typically represented in English with the suffix –er (singer, bak-er, preach-er, etc.). How one understands the preposition
"before" influences one's understanding of the word prophet.
In the oldest literature, *before* was understood spatially, as in
before/in front of an audience, so that the prophet is someone
who speaks publicly, proclaims, and announces to others. In
this sense, the prophet was a forth-teller, in that the speech is
going forth into other ears and hearts. In later literature, perhaps
beginning with the turn of the millennium into the Common Era,
before began to be understood temporally, as in before/earlier
than an event happened, so that the prophet is someone who
speaks about something in advance. In this sense, the prophet

was a fore-teller, in that the speech is forecasting the future. Certain forms of literature were constructed with particular events deliberately set in the distant past so as to be used by the author as proof that those events "predict" the current situation. So, for example, after Cyrus has conquered Babylon and released the captives, the prophet Isaiah can write that God will shortly bring about the release by means of King Cyrus. When this literature is disconnected from its original moorings, the sense of prophecy as prediction takes over. This sense has predominated in the New Testament, for example, as the authors of the Gospels interpreted ancient prophecies in light of the Christ event. The notion of ancient prophets as predictors, in the sense of fortune-tellers, dominates the contemporary mindset, an understanding not held in high esteem in the modern, scientific worldview. On the other hand, moderns do seem to value those among us who speak prophetically, by which we usually mean speaking a word of truth that may be hard to hear. Speaking prophetically in recent memory were civil rights leaders such as Martin Luther King Jr. and environmental activists such as Rachel Carson. As we will see, the Old Testament prophets were not so much predictors of the future in the fortune-telling sense as they were speakers of truth in a particular socio-historical context.

The Greek word *prophetes* is always used to translate the most common Hebrew word for prophet, *nabi'*. The origin of the Hebrew word is not as clear as the Greek, although words with the same consonants in other ancient Near Eastern languages are related to speaking. For example, the Assyrian word *nabu* means to call, proclaim, or appoint to an office. The root *nabi'* in its verbal and nominal form occurs over 500 times in the Old Testament. Two other less frequent Hebrew words indicate a connection between prophecy and visions, *ro'eh*, "one who sees," and *chozeh*, "one who has visions."

The Prophetic Vocation

Universally in the ancient Near East, prophets understood themselves to have a 'vocation' more than an 'occupation.' The word 'vocation' comes from the Latin verb that means "to call," often implying a divine call. Rather than doing something that simply 'occupies' time, the prophet 'calls' to others because of the 'call' received from the deity.

Connection between Deity and Prophet

A famous example of the divine speaking through a human voice is the oracle at Delphi in ancient Greece, active since at least the beginning of the first millennium BCE and famous far beyond Greek borders. A person, also known as Pythia in the literature, announced the divine will, usually in response to a specific question. Ancient texts call this role *promantis*, the combination of *pro*, "before," and *mantis*, "a state of frenzy," as in the English word "manic." The *promantis* announced the divine will to the questioner as a result of a state of frenzy, now supposed to be the result of inhaling intoxicating vapors. Ancient texts also describe a *prophetes* at the oracle of Delphi. Sometimes this is used to describe the Pythia, emphasizing the role as a speaking conduit of the deity. At other times, the texts point to a separate individual at the shrine whose task was to render the Pythian speech intelligible to the questioner.

We noted above that the Hebrew word *nabi'*, the most common word for "prophet" in the Old Testament, is semantically related to the Assyrian word *nabu*, a word related to speaking. Interestingly, the word *nabu* is the name of an important Mesopotamian deity whose main temple was in Borsippa, about 11 miles southwest of Babylon. Nabu was known as the scribe of the chief god Marduk and, as such, inscribed the fate of all humans into the sacred records, including the person's length of life. As such an important figure, the worship of Nabu spread beyond

Mesopotamia to Egypt, Syria, and Anatolia (modern Turkey), and lasted even into the Common Era, as attested by excavated inscriptions. He is often depicted with his writing symbols, the clay tablet and the stylus, and standing on a dragon, symbolizing his power over deadly forces. His popularity is indicated by the frequency of human names that incorporate the divine name Nabu (or Nebu), including the familiar Babylonian king who destroyed Jerusalem, Nebuchadnezzar. The Assyrian god Nabu and the Assyrian verb *nabu* (to proclaim) may illumine a distinguishing mark of prophecy in the ancient world: any proclamation done by the prophet is done in the name of the divine.

The divine–prophet connectedness is described in the Old Testament in terms of the *ruach* of God. The Hebrew word can mean breath or wind or spirit, typically envisioning an empowering or animating force. The use at this point of a lower-case *s* for the word spirit is deliberate, because a capital *S* may imply to some readers a person of the Trinitarian Godhead. Although some have interpreted Old Testament language of the spirit in that way, the Old Testament texts make no such claim themselves. The claim made in the Old Testament is that the phenomenon of true prophecy is intimately interconnected with the *ruach* of God. Four extended episodes and a few scattered verses will illustrate the point.

After leaving Mt Sinai at the command of God in order to proceed to the Promised Land, the people complain about the inconvenience of traveling in the wilderness, first in generalized terms (Num 11:1) and then in specific terms. "The rabble among them had a strong craving; and the Israelites also wept again, and said, 'If only we had meat to eat! We remember the fish we used to eat in Egypt for nothing, the cucumbers, the melons, the leeks, the onions, and the garlic; but now our strength is dried up, and there is nothing at all but this manna to look at'" (Num 11:4–6). Talk about revisionist history! How can they talk about this smorgasbord of food in Egypt of all places, where they worked as slaves making bricks without straw in the hot desert sun? Surely they remember that they didn't eat in Egypt "for nothing"! Moses must have experienced the same exasperation I feel every time I read this text, because he complains to God about his frustration: "Where am I to get meat to give to all this people? For they come weeping to me and say, 'Give us meat to eat!' I am not able to carry all this people alone, for they are too heavy for me" (Num 11:13–14). So Moses is instructed to choose seventy elders and take them to the tent of meeting outside the camp, where the Lord will solve the problem. "Then the LORD came down in the cloud and spoke to him, and took some of the spirit [*ruach*] that was on him and put it on the seventy elders; and when the spirit rested upon them, they prophesied [verbal form of *nabi'*]" (Num 11:25). The text clearly claims that prophecy is a direct result of the spirit resting on them. In fact, a strong, causal connection between the spirit of God and the act of prophecy is one of the points of the vignette that immediately follows (besides discouraging tattle-tales).

> Two men remained in the camp, one named Eldad, and the other named Medad, and the spirit [*ruach*] rested on them; they were among those registered, but they had not gone out to the tent, and so they prophesied [verbal form of *nabi'*] in the camp. And a young man ran and told Moses, "Eldad and Medad are prophesying [verbal form of *nabi'*] in the camp." And Joshua son of Nun, the assistant of Moses, one of his chosen men, said, "My lord Moses, stop them!" But Moses said to him, "Are you jealous for my sake? Would that all the LORD's people were prophets [*nabi'*], and that the LORD would put his spirit [*ruach*] on them!" And Moses and the elders of Israel returned to the camp. (Num 11:26–30)

The second episode connecting prophets and the spirit of God is in 1 Samuel 10, when Saul has just been secretly anointed by Samuel as the first king of Israel. On Saul's return trip home, "a band of prophets [*nabi'*] met him; and the spirit [*ruach*] of God possessed him, and he fell into a prophetic frenzy [verbal form of *nabi'*] along with them. When all who knew him before saw how he prophesied [verbal form of *nabi'*] with the prophets [*nabi'*], the people said to one another, 'What has come over the son of Kish? Is Saul also among the prophets [*nabi'*]?'" (1 Sam 10:10–11). His behavior seems to have been so unusual as to warrant comment from those who knew him as a more sedate man. In fact, this is exactly what Samuel had said would happen to Saul: "After that you shall come to Gibeath-elohim, at the place where the Philistine garrison is; there, as you come to the town, you will meet a band of prophets [*nabi'*] coming down from the shrine with harp, tambourine, flute, and lyre playing in front of them; they will be in a prophetic frenzy [verbal form of *nabi'*]. Then the spirit [*ruach*] of the LORD will possess you, and you will be in a prophetic frenzy [verbal form of *nabi'*] along with them and be turned into a different person" (1 Sam 10:5–6). Apparently we are to understand that dealing with the Philistine threat will require the spirit of God resting on Saul more than the force of armies.

The next episode also involves King Saul, this time as one possessed by an evil spirit from the Lord and intent on killing his rival David. David fled Saul's palace and went with Samuel to the neighborhood of Naioth in the city of Ramah. "Then Saul sent messengers to take David. When they saw the company of the prophets [*nabi'*] in a frenzy [verbal form of *nabi'*], with Samuel standing in charge of them, the spirit [*ruach*] of God came upon the messengers of Saul, and they also fell into a prophetic frenzy [verbal form of *nabi'*]. When Saul was told, he sent other messengers, and they also fell into a frenzy [verbal form of *nabi'*]. Saul sent messengers again the third time, and they also fell into a frenzy [verbal form of *nabi'*]" (1 Sam 19:20–21). Unhappy with the inability of his messengers to capture David, Saul himself goes to find David. "And the spirit [*ruach*] of God came upon him. As he was going, he fell into a prophetic frenzy [verbal form of *nabi'*], until he came to Naioth in Ramah. He too stripped off his clothes, and he too fell into a frenzy [verbal form of *nabi'*] before Samuel. He lay naked all that day and all that night. Therefore it is said, 'Is Saul also among the prophets [*nabi'*]?'" (1 Sam 19:23–24). Scholars have suggested that each story may come from a different traditional source in order to explain the apparently well-known question, "Is Saul also among the prophets?" No matter the source, both episodes connect the spirit of God and prophetic frenzy characterized by unusual behavior. Here we see similarities with the oracle at Delphi, the *promantis*, and individuals described in texts from other surrounding cultures like Egypt and Syria. The Hebrew bands of prophets are frequently termed "sons of prophets" in the texts, perhaps indicating a familiar profession. Near the beginning of the captivating story of Elijah being taken into heaven in a whirlwind, "sons of the prophets" come out from both Bethel and Jericho to communicate with Elisha about the upcoming departure of his master.

The setting for the final extended episode is a battle plan against Syria initiated by Ahab, king of the northern kingdom of Israel in the mid-ninth century BCE, in which he asks Jehoshaphat, king of the southern kingdom of Judah, to participate. Ahab inquires of about 400 prophets, who assure him of a successful outcome. Skeptical of the prophecy, Jehoshaphat asks for yet another opinion. "The king of Israel said to Jehoshaphat, 'There is still one other by whom we may inquire of the LORD, Micaiah son of Imlah; but I hate him, for he never prophesies anything favorable about me, but only disaster'" (1 Kgs 22:8). When the prophet is summoned, he unpredictably prophesies victory. But when pressed by the king to tell the truth, he prophesies defeat at the hands of Syria, as King Ahab had expected. So the prophet justifies his prophecy of defeat by recounting a vision.

> I saw the LORD sitting on his throne, with all the host of heaven standing beside him to the right and to the left of him. And the LORD said, 'Who will entice Ahab, so that he may go up and fall at Ramoth-gilead [in Syria]?' Then one said one thing, and another said another, until a spirit [*ruach*] came forward and stood before the LORD,

> saying, 'I will entice him.' 'How?' the LORD asked him. He replied, 'I will go out and be a lying spirit [*ruach*] in the mouth of all his prophets [*nabi'*].' Then the LORD said, 'You are to entice him, and you shall succeed; go out and do it.' So you see, the LORD has put a lying spirit [*ruach*] in the mouth of all these your prophets [*nabi'*]; the LORD has decreed disaster for you. (1 Kgs 22:19–23)

Besides illustrating the tight connection between the spirit and prophecy, this episode introduces us to the persistent question throughout Israel's history of true prophecy vs. false prophecy, a question to which we will return soon.

The four episodes explored thus far may reasonably be attributed to the early periods of Israel's history, even if their memorialization in writing came much later. In the story of the mantle passing from Elijah to Elisha, a company of prophets who had come from Jericho certify Elisha's prophetic credentials by saying, "The spirit [*ruach*] of Elijah rests on Elisha" (2 Kgs 3:15). There are also verses from exilic and post-exilic texts that reflect the enduring connection between the spirit of God and prophets. When Ezra is recounting the history of Israel from Abram to the present day (c. 400 BCE), he says, "Many years you were patient with them, and warned them by your spirit [*ruach*] through your prophets [*nabi'*]; yet they would not listen. Therefore you handed them over to the peoples of the lands" (Neh 9:30). Zechariah says essentially the same thing: "They made their hearts adamant in order not to hear the law and the words that the LORD of hosts had sent by his spirit [*ruach*] through the former prophets [*nabi'*]. Therefore great wrath came from the LORD of hosts" (Zech 7:12). Ezekiel connects his calling as a prophet with the spirit of God coming upon him. "And when he [the Lord] spoke to me, a spirit [*ruach*] entered into me and set me on my feet; and I heard him speaking to me . . . 'The descendants [of Israel] are impudent and stubborn. I am sending you to them, and you shall say to them, "Thus says the Lord GOD." Whether they hear or refuse to hear (for they are a rebellious house), they shall know that there has been a prophet [*nabi'*] among them'" (Ezek 2:2, 4-5). Throughout the book of Ezekiel, the spirit of God transports the prophet, including to the familiar valley of dry bones. "The hand of the LORD came upon me, and he brought me out by the spirit [*ruach*] of the LORD and set me down in the middle of a valley; it was full of bones" (Ezek 37:1). "Then he said to me, 'Prophesy to the breath [*ruach*], prophesy, mortal, and say to the breath [*ruach*]: Thus says the Lord GOD: Come from the four winds [plural *ruach*], O breath [*ruach*], and breathe upon these slain, that they may live.' I prophesied as he commanded me, and the breath [*ruach*] came into them, and they lived, and stood on their feet, a vast multitude" (Ezek 37:9-10). This text demonstrates a double-coincidence of spirit and prophecy: the spirit animates the prophet and the prophet's prophecy to the spirit animates the dry bones. The prophet is no longer the vessel whose primary role is to contain the spirit of God, but the conduit of the spirit of God into the world to animate others. Something like this is also seen in the words of the prophet Joel describing an eschatological vision of the Day of the Lord: "Then afterward I will pour out my spirit [*ruach*] on all flesh; your sons and your daughters shall prophesy [verbal form of *nabi'*], your old men shall dream dreams, and your young men shall see visions. Even on the male and female slaves, in those days, I will pour out my spirit [*ruach*]" (Joel 2:28-29). These words are quoted in Acts 2, with the additional phrase at the end, "and they shall prophesy" (Acts 2:17-18) as evidence of the coming of the Holy Spirit.

Social Location of Prophets

In the modern mind, the figure of the prophet has been greatly influenced by the depiction of John the Baptizer in the Gospel narratives of Matthew, Mark, and Luke. The remarkable circumstances of John's birth are recounted in the first chapter of Luke's Gospel. The astonished neighbors say, "What then will this child become?" (Luke 1:66). The narrator concludes this portion of John's story, "The child grew and became strong in spirit, and he was in the wilderness until the day he appeared publicly to Israel" (Luke 1:80). The Gospel of Matthew supplies further details: "Now John wore clothing of camel's hair with a leather belt around his waist, and his food was locusts and wild honey" (Matt 3:4). Popular imagination has reveled in this depiction of John the Baptizer, and by extension, ancient prophets. We imagine an Old Testament prophet as a solitary individual outcast from the community, wandering in the wilderness, foraging for food and shelter, ranting about the wrath of God. No doubt, there is some truth in this understanding of prophets as individuals going against the grain of polite society. On the other hand, the very fact that we know anything at all about Old Testament prophets means that someone recorded their stories and words. To state the obvious, they had enough social status to be remembered in the oral tradition and subsequent written record. So while some prophets were certainly on the periphery of social power structures, their peripheral location was still within the realm of the community.

Other prophets, by contrast, seem to have exercised their vocation at the seat of social power at the royal court. We have already been introduced to this type of prophet in the story of Ahab and Jehoshaphat (1 Kgs 22:1–23), when Ahab gathered prophets to inquire about the upcoming battle. When the prophet Micaiah ben Imlah is recounting his vision, he explains to Ahab, "So you see, the LORD has put a lying spirit in the mouth of all these your prophets" (1 Kgs 22:22). He explicitly calls the 400 prophets consulted by Ahab *your* prophets. Likewise, in the same vision report, the spirit who stands before the Lord to offer his services says, "I will go out and be a lying spirit in the mouth of all his prophets" (1 Kgs 22:23). Here the prophets are called *his* prophets, that is, belonging to the royal court of Ahab. Presumably, the prophets are attached to the king's service precisely to be called upon to render a verdict in times like this. Interestingly, the text does not specify that they are prophets *of the Lord*. In fact, as this story follows on the story of the prophets of Ba'al and Elijah on Mt Carmel (1 Kings 18), it makes more sense for Jehoshaphat to ask for another opinion precisely because these 400 prophets are not prophets of the Lord, but prophets of Ba'al, an important Canaanite god. As a faithful follower of Israel's God, Jehoshaphat would not have trusted the prophets of Ba'al. In 1 Kgs 18:19, Elijah calls upon Ahab to gather at Mt Carmel "with the four hundred fifty prophets of Baal and the four hundred prophets of Asherah [a female Canaanite deity], who eat at Jezebel's table." The final phrase of that verse referring to Queen Jezebel indicates that the prophets were in the employ of the royal court.

David is remembered in the biblical texts as having direct access to two prophets. The prophet Gad appears to have been associated with David in his early exploits before he became established as king. Regularly referred to as *nabi'*, in one verse Gad is called "the prophet Gad, David's seer [*chozeh*]" (2 Sam 24:11). In this verse we see not only the direct connection with an important political figure, but also another title for the role of prophet. The prophet Nathan is instrumental as an intermediary between God and King David when the king initially wants to build a temple in Jerusalem (2 Samuel 7). More to the point is the narrator's comment regarding Nathan near the end of David's reign. As David becomes weakened with his advanced age, his eldest living son Adonijah takes the necessary steps to assume the throne. "Adonijah sacrificed sheep, oxen, and fatted cattle by the stone Zoheleth, which is beside En-rogel, and he invited all his brothers, the king's sons, and all the royal officials of Judah, but he did not invite the prophet Nathan or Benaiah [an army commander] or the warriors or his brother Solomon" (1 Kgs 1:9–10). Nathan is specifically excluded from the "royal officials of Judah" invited to the feast. In the discussion of prophets with direct access to the king or temple, we may also include a woman called *nabi'ah*, the feminine form of *nabi'*, the masculine word for prophet. The prophetess Huldah is consulted about the 'Book of the Law' discovered during temple renovations. King Josiah sends a delegation that includes the royal secretary, the high priest, and three other high officials to "the prophetess Huldah the wife of Shallum son of Tikvah, son of Harhas, keeper of the wardrobe; she resided in Jerusalem in the Second Quarter, where they consulted her" (2 Kgs 22:14). We can completely understand the desire of kings to have easy access to prophets, since prophets can provide answers to questions that kings have.

Another example of a prophet with social power is Deborah. "At that time Deborah, a prophetess [*nabi'ah*,], wife of Lappidoth, was judging Israel. She used to sit under the palm of Deborah between Ramah and Bethel in the hill country of Ephraim; and the Israelites came up to her for judgment" (Judg 4:4–5). Whether Deborah's designation as prophetess is attributed to her resolving disputes for Israelites who came to her or to her role in the impending battle with the Canaanite general Sisera is uncertain.

Most of the prophets in the Old Testament are not what we might call "professional" prophets, if that means being supported by the royal court or joining the ancient version of a prophetic guild. Amos specifically distances himself from this category when he explains, "I am no prophet [*nabi'*], nor a prophet's son [*ben nabi'*]; but I am a herdsman, and a dresser of sycamore trees, and the LORD took me from following the flock, and the LORD said to me, 'Go, prophesy [verbal form of *nabi'*] to my people Israel'" (Amos 7:14–15). The majority of prophets in the Old Testament seem to be individuals who are somehow overwhelmed by a compulsion to communicate a divine word, either in speech or action.

True and False Prophets

As individuals claim to be overcome by the spirit of the Lord and utter prophecies, the issue of discernment between true and false prophets becomes important. First, the Old Testament understands a false prophet to be any person who speaks in the name of the God of Israel without having been called to do so. Deuteronomy puts it succinctly: "But any prophet who speaks in the name of other gods, or who presumes to speak in my name a word that I have not commanded the prophet to speak—that prophet shall die" (Deut 18:20). In Ezekiel, these persons are said to "prophesy out of their own imagination: 'Hear the word of the LORD!'" and "follow their own spirit" (Ezek 13:2–3). "They have envisioned falsehood and lying divination; they say, 'Says the LORD,' when the LORD has not sent them, and yet they wait for the fulfillment of their word! Have you not seen a false vision or uttered a lying divination, when you have said, 'Says the LORD,' even though I did not speak?" (Ezek 13:6–7). Second, a false prophet is one who may in fact be called by God, but speaks a word other than the one God has given. Some texts recognize that prophets may be bribed into giving a false prophecy. For example, the prophet Micah says, "its [Jerusalem's] prophets give oracles for money" (Mic 3:11) and condemns those who "lead my [God's] people astray, who cry 'Peace' when they have something to eat, but declare war against those who put nothing into their mouths" (Mic 3:5). Likewise, Jeremiah announces, "For from the least to the greatest of them, everyone is greedy for unjust gain; and from prophet to priest, everyone deals falsely. They have treated the wound of my people carelessly, saying, 'Peace, peace,' when there is no peace" (Jer 6:13–14). In the final analysis, the discernment of false prophets demands the passage of time. As explained in Deut 6:21–22, "You may say to yourself, 'How can we recognize a word that the LORD has not spoken?' If a prophet speaks in the name of the LORD but the thing does not take place or prove true, it is a word that the LORD has not spoken. The prophet has spoken it presumptuously; do not be frightened by it."

Forms of Prophetic Speech

Readers of the Bible have long noted differing literary forms in its books. Much scholarship in the nineteenth and twentieth centuries was devoted to identifying ancient genres of literature, because different genres elicit different interpretations. For example, a text that begins, "Dear Sir" will be read in a way that will not be appropriate for a text that begins, "Hey Sally!" Likewise, if a reader sees, "And the leader said, 'Dearly beloved, we are gathered here today . . . ,'" the reader knows to expect to encounter the cultural setting of a wedding. In this section, we explore some of the most frequent genres of prophetic speech.

Call Narrative

The sense of divine call seems to be the determining factor for most of the prophets in the Old Testament. Narration of the divine selection of the prophet typically follows a standard literary pattern, known as the 'Call Narrative' genre. Typically, the Call Narrative contains the four elements discussed below, although there are plenty of prophets in the Old Testament whose divine call is not narrated at all.

1. Awareness of the divine presence. The most common language for a person's super-awareness of the divine presence is, "The word of the LORD came to [Name]" (for example, 1 Sam 15:10 to Samuel; 2 Sam 7:4 to Nathan; 1 Kgs 18:1 to Elijah; Hos 1:1 to Hosea; Joel 1:1 to Joel; and many more). The Hebrew word translated into English as "came" is the past tense form of the verbal root *hayah*, a word that means "to be(come), to happen." The sense is something like, "The word of the LORD happened to" a certain person. The details of exactly how the word of the Lord "happened to" the person are not generally explained; the *fact* that the word of the Lord happened seems to be more important than the *means* by which the word of the Lord happened. In some cases, the text indicates that the person had some kind

of vision in which the divine presence is mediated. For example, "the vision of Obadiah" (Obad 1), or "The book of the vision of Nahum" (Nah 1:1), or "In the year that King Uzziah died, I saw the Lord sitting upon a throne, high and lofty, and the hem of his robe filled the temple" (Isa 6:1). In an interesting combination, the book of Amos begins, "The words of Amos, . . . which he saw concerning Israel" (1:1). Where we would expect Amos to *hear* the words [of the Lord], the narrator reports that Amos *sees* the words, alerting the reader to the five visions that Amos will have in later chapters.

2. Identification of person as a prophet of the divine. As step two, the divine word selects the person as a prophetic messenger. For example, "Before I formed you in the womb I knew you, and before you were born I consecrated you; I appointed you a prophet to the nations" (Jer 1:5). At this point, the task to be undertaken may also be articulated. For example, "Now the word of the LORD came to Jonah son of Amittai, saying, 'Go at once to Nineveh, that great city, and cry out against it; for their wickedness has come up before me'" (Jonah 1:1-2).

3. Response from the prophet, often an objection to the call. Steps one and two seem to indicate that in the world of ancient Israel, one did not volunteer to be a prophet. Rather, the call to be a prophet was something thrust upon a person without consideration of whether the call was welcomed or not. So it should not be surprising that many of the people called as prophets in the Old Testament voice some kind of objection to the divine call. Some familiar examples will illustrate the point. Jeremiah protests, "Ah, Lord GOD! Truly I do not know how to speak, for I am only a boy" (Jer 1:6). Upon seeing his vision of the Divine King, Isaiah blurts out, "Woe is me! I am lost, for I am a man of unclean lips, and I live among a people of unclean lips; yet my eyes have seen the King, the LORD of hosts!" (Isa 6:5). Jonah, hearing God's direction to go to Ninevah over 600 miles to the east, immediately boarded a ship sailing west towards Spain (Jonah 1:3). Moses, remembered in the biblical canon as a prophet *par excellence*,

voices multiple objections to God's call to go to Pharaoh and demand the release of the Hebrew slaves (Exodus 3–5). We should add at this point that a prophet's objection to being called by God is not necessarily limited to the initial encounter with the divine. Jeremiah is remembered in the biblical text as lamenting his prophetic vocation on more than one occasion. Jeremiah accuses God of failing to protect him when he prophesied God's word. "Your words were found, and I ate them, and your words became to me a joy and the delight of my heart; for I am called by your name, O LORD, God of hosts. I did not sit in the company of merrymakers, nor did I rejoice; under the weight of your hand I sat alone, for you had filled me with indignation. Why is my pain unceasing, my wound incurable, refusing to be healed? Truly, you are to me like a deceitful brook, like waters that fail" (Jer 15:16–18). After being beaten and put in stocks for his prophecies, Jeremiah lashes out at God with poignant honesty.

> O LORD, you have enticed me, and I was enticed; you have overpowered me, and you have prevailed. I have become a laughingstock all day long; everyone mocks me. For whenever I speak, I must cry out, I must shout, "Violence and destruction!" For the word of the LORD has become for me a reproach and derision all day long. If I say, "I will not mention him, or speak any more in his name," then within me there is something like a burning fire shut up in my bones; I am weary with holding it in, and I cannot. (Jer 20:7–9)

4. Reassurance by the divine to overcome the objection. If an objection is registered, action is undertaken by the divine to remedy the situation. When Jeremiah demurs due to his young age, the Lord said to him, "Do not say, 'I am only a boy'; for you shall go to all to whom I send you, and you shall speak whatever I command you" (Jer 1:7). There's no available remedy for Jeremiah's young age; rather, the remedy is that Jeremiah will speak the Lord's words and not his own. Isaiah acknowledges his impurity ("unclean lips") and, therefore, his unworthiness

to see the Divine King. The remedy is swift and effective: "Then one of the seraphs flew to me, holding a live coal that had been taken from the altar with a pair of tongs. The seraph touched my mouth with it and said: 'Now that this has touched your lips, your guilt has departed and your sin is blotted out'" (Isa 6:6–7). The use of fire as a purifying agent was well known in the ancient world, here used in a ritual context. Jonah's action of running the opposite direction leads to the extended action in the first two chapters of the book, a familiar story to most. Chosen by lot as the one responsible for the tempest at sea, Jonah is tossed overboard, swallowed by a big fish, and finally vomited onto the dry land, all presented as the Lord's reaction to Jonah's disobedience. The reader realizes how effective the remedy has been; "The word of the LORD came to Jonah a second time, saying, 'Get up, go to Nineveh, that great city, and proclaim to it the message that I tell you.' So Jonah set out and went to Nineveh, according to the word of the LORD" (Jonah 3:1–3a). In the extended narrative of the call of Moses, every objection raised by Moses is remedied by God, including signs and wonders that impress not only Moses, but are likely to impress the people as well and thereby confirm his call.

Messenger Speech

The divine call and commissioning authorizes the prophet to speak in the name of God. As we saw above, the divine remedy for objections often includes reminding the prophet that the word to be forth-told is specifically the word of the Lord, not the prophet's own word. Messengers were regularly used by kings or other political functionaries to communicate with their subjects. The idea of royal messenger is behind the biblical notion of angels, who function in the oldest texts as God's messengers. In Hebrew, the word *mala'k* can be translated as either messenger (if sent by the king) or as angel (if sent by God). All messengers in the ancient world memorized the message word for word and were understood to be speaking as the one sending the message and with that same authority. The cultural phenomenon of royal messengers is adopted by the prophets, who are understood as messengers of the Divine King.

The most common literary form used by messengers involves three steps. The first step is the commissioning of the messenger by the king. The king gives explicit instruction to the messenger regarding to whom he is being sent and what exactly he is to say when he gets there. In the instructions lies the "messenger formula"—"thus says King [Name]." This simple phrase carries within it all the authority of the king. "Thus" means "in these exact words and backed by all the power of the king." The second step was the transition of the messenger from the king to the intended audience. The final step is the delivery of the message, introduced by the messenger formula "Thus says King [Name]" and announced verbatim. Often the message is composed in two parts: a report and a summons. The report describes what the audience has or has not done to warrant a royal message and serves as the reason for the summons. The summons is the royal command that is the result of the report. Here is a hypothetical royal message that illustrates the standard genre.

> Then King Marty summoned the royal messenger and said, "Go to the mayor of Gettysburg and say, 'Thus says King Marty: You have failed to pay your taxes on time. Therefore, pay all you owe right now, or I will come and take all your stored silver.'" So the messenger went to the mayor of Gettysburg, arriving the next day. And the messenger said, "Thus says King Marty: You have failed to pay your taxes on time. Therefore, pay all you owe right now, or I will come and take all your stored silver." So the mayor paid all his taxes right away, for he feared King Marty.

Note that the messenger speaks in the first person, as if it were the king speaking. This rhetorical device emphasizes the authority residing in the messenger. In the prophetic books, first person speech often makes it difficult to distinguish whether the prophet is speaking as prophet or as divine messenger. Also note the emphatic "therefore" that transitions between the report and the summons. Immediately following the "therefore" is the announcement of judgment. In this hypothetical example, King Marty is giving the mayor of Gettysburg a chance to avoid the judgment by taking immediate action to pay the amount owed.

Once we understand the standard format of the messenger speech, we can easily see how the form is appropriated for prophetic judgment speech. As noted above, the prophetic call narrative serves as the commissioning of the prophet as the divine messenger. So the prophetic judgment speech typically begins with the report. Consider the following judgment speech in the book of Micah.

> Alas for those who devise wickedness and evil deeds on their beds! When the morning dawns, they perform it, because it is in their power. They covet fields, and seize them; houses, and take them away; they oppress householder and house, people and their inheritance. Therefore thus says the LORD: Now, I am devising against this family an evil from which you cannot remove your necks; and you shall not walk haughtily, for it will be an evil time. On that day they shall take up a taunt song against you, and wail with bitter lamentation, and say, "We are utterly ruined; the LORD alters the inheritance of my people; how he removes it from me! Among our captors he parcels out our fields." (Mic 2:1–4)

Notice the transition between the report and the summons by means of "therefore," immediately followed by the messenger formula "thus says the LORD." Commonly found in prophetic judgment speech is a correlation between the accusation and the punishment. Here, the people devise evil, so the Lord is devising evil; the people covet and seize fields, so the Lord distributes their fields to their captors; the people oppress others' inheritance, so the Lord alters their inheritance.

The messenger speech genre also helps us understand the prophet as forth-teller more than fore-teller. Consider a parent who says to a child, "You are running with scissors. Therefore, you will get hurt." In saying this, the parent does not normally mean to predict that the child will get hurt, as if the parent were telling the future unknown to anyone else. The parent generally means that if current behavior continues, there are likely consequences from that behavior. The parent is forth-telling, not fore-telling, the future. So it is with the Old Testament prophet. The prophet, speaking for God, analyzes the current context and announces the consequences of continuing current behavior. Sometimes, the objectionable behavior has gotten to the point of no return, so that there is no chance to avert the upcoming punishment. At other times, the prophet pleads with the people to change so as to avoid the otherwise inevitable punishment.

But prophets are not only announcers of doom and gloom, although certainly there is considerable judgment proclaimed by the Old Testament prophets. The prophets are also God's messengers of hope and salvation. Although the messenger's speech format was probably also used to craft announcements of salvation, the elements are less structured than in the announcement of judgment. Notably, the report is omitted. Whereas the report is critical to the judgment speech as an accusation of behavior justifying the punishment about to be announced, no such element is needed in salvation speech. In other words, there is no human behavior that justifies an announcement of salvation by God through the prophetic messenger. By omitting the report and moving directly to the summons (to salvation), the reader cannot help but understand salvation as a gracious, undeserved gift of God. A clear example is Isa 43:1: "But now thus says the LORD, he who created you, O Jacob, he who formed you, O Israel: Do not fear, for I have redeemed you; I have called you by name, you are mine."

Other Forms of Prophetic Announcements

Limitations of space prevent a full discussion of types of prophetic speech. Rather, two general forms are examined: specialized types of judgment announcements and symbolic actions. "Woe oracles" are judgment announcements that begin with the Hebrew word *hoy*, translated in English as either "woe" or "alas." Apparently, the word *hoy* was primarily used as a funeral lament, the equivalent of crying over the dead body at the grave. So, for example, "He laid the body in his own grave; and they mourned over him, saying, 'Alas [*hoy*], my brother!'" (1 Kgs 13:30). When the prophet shows up and announces 'Woe,' the consequences are about to be deadly. Woe oracles are often used to announce judgment to foreign nations for their apostasy and/or evil treatment of Israel. Another specialized type of judgment announcement is the "trial speech" or "disputation." The prophet summons the audience as the defendant at a judicial proceeding, with God as the plaintiff, leveling charges against the audience. For example, "Hear what the LORD says: Rise, plead your case before the mountains, and let the hills hear your voice. Hear, you mountains, the controversy of the LORD, and you enduring foundations of the earth; for the LORD has a controversy with his people, and he will contend with Israel" (Mic 6:1–2). What is often left unsaid is that, in addition to being the plaintiff, God is also the judge.

Sometimes the prophets are messengers for God without using any words at all, relying on their actions to interpret the divine message to the audience. Three examples will suffice. The first example is the prophet Hosea, active in the northern kingdom in the eighth century BCE. The narration of his initial call is instructive: "When the LORD first spoke through Hosea, the LORD said to Hosea, 'Go, take for yourself a wife of whoredom and have children of whoredom, for the land commits great whoredom by forsaking the LORD'" (Hos 1:2). The author mentions that the Lord is speaking directly *to* Hosea with a command to marry a prostitute and *through* Hosea to the nation at large.

The children of this union are given symbolic names: "God sows [seed]," "not pitied," and "not my people." Later, Hosea is called to (re)marry a prostitute: "The LORD said to me again, 'Go, love a woman who has a lover and is an adulteress, just as the LORD loves the people of Israel, though they turn to other gods and love raisin cakes'" (Hos 3:1). Even as Hosea is called to love one who is unfaithful, so God continues to love unfaithful Israel.

The second example of symbolic prophetic action is the prophet Ezekiel, active in the early sixth century before and after the exile of 587 BCE. Ezekiel is instructed by God to pretend to be an exile leaving the city of Jerusalem, so that the people will realize the gravity of the situation.

> Therefore, mortal, prepare for yourself an exile's baggage, and go into exile by day in their sight; you shall go like an exile from your place to another place in their sight . . . You shall bring out your baggage by day in their sight, as baggage for exile; and you shall go out yourself at evening in their sight, as those do who go into exile. Dig through the wall in their sight, and carry the baggage through it. In their sight you shall lift the baggage on your shoulder, and carry it out in the dark; you shall cover your face, so that you may not see the land; for I have made you a sign for the house of Israel . . . Say to them, "Thus says the Lord GOD: This oracle concerns the prince in Jerusalem and all the house of Israel in it." Say, "I am a sign for you: as I have done, so shall it be done to them; they shall go into exile, into captivity." (Ezek 12:2–3a; 4–6, 10–11)

Finally, the prophet Jeremiah uses a real estate transaction to bring a divine word of hope to the people even as the Babylonian army is besieging Jerusalem in 587 BCE. Jeremiah, imprisoned in the royal palace for prophesying Babylonian victory, reports, "The word of the LORD came [happened] to me: Hanamel son of your uncle Shallum is going to come to you and say, 'Buy my field that is at Anathoth, for the right of redemption by purchase is yours'" (Jer 32:6–7). After Jeremiah buys the field, he reports, "Thus says the LORD of hosts, the God of Israel:

Take these deeds, both this sealed deed of purchase and this open deed, and put them in an earthenware jar, in order that they may last for a long time. For thus says the LORD of hosts, the God of Israel: Houses and fields and vineyards shall again be bought in this land" (Jer 32:14–15). In the face of impending destruction by a foreign army, Jeremiah's purchase of land offers assurance of restoration to the land in the future.

The Message of the Prophets

Prophets were people overcome by the spirit of God, called to speak the word of the Lord about the future consequences of behavior at that time and in that place. That is, each prophet was speaking the truth in a particular social and historical context and, as such, deserves to be interpreted individually. At the same time, however, we can recognize certain overarching themes that are common to the prophetic voices in the Old Testament.

Covenant Faithfulness

The Old Testament describes the relationship between God and Israel as a covenant relationship (Hebrew *berit*), wherein both parties are permanently bound to one another by something like a treaty or contract. Political treaties were common in the ancient Near East, so it is no surprise that the divine–human relationship would be envisioned using the treaty metaphor. Multiple covenants are enacted in the Old Testament, some between various individuals or groups of people and some with God and individuals or groups of people. We may think of the covenants with Noah (Genesis 9), Abraham (Genesis 15, 17), and David (2 Samuel 7). In these familiar covenants, God promises various benefits for keeping the covenant: a ban on destruction of the earth by water, land, numerous progeny, dynastic kingship. But the most important covenant in the Old Testament is the Sinai

Covenant (with a capital *C*), by which we mean the legislation enacted between God and the escaped Hebrew slaves led by Moses, recorded in Exodus 20 to Leviticus 27 and recapitulated in Deuteronomy. Even though the laws were promulgated in multiple time periods and recorded by multiple authors, in the final form of the Pentateuch, all these laws are understood as originating at Mt Sinai through the agency of Moses. The core of the covenantal promise is: "I will be your God and you will be my people" (see, for example, Exod 6:7; Lev 26:12; Jer 7:23; 11:4; 30:22; Ezek 36:28). Literally, the Hebrew says, "I will become God for you and you will become people for me." The language of "become" indicates a process of growing in relationship not immediately obvious in the English. Also, the Hebrew indicates the benefit of the relationship: God for you and people for me. There is willingness in the relationship that may be obscured by the English pronouns *your* and *my*. The biblical notion of covenant (*berit*) is essentially relational and beneficial in nature.

In general, the prophets do not use the word *berit* frequently to describe God's relationship with God's people. They do, however, criticize the people for behaviors that clearly violate the covenant relationship, and they exhort the people to live in ways that honor the covenant relationship. So the divine covenant is the backdrop for prophetic speech, whether explicitly signaled by the use of the word *berit* or not. For example, Hosea engages in trial speech to accuse the people of breaking at least some of the Ten Commandments. "Hear the word of the LORD, O people of Israel; for the LORD has an indictment against the inhabitants of the land. There is no faithfulness or loyalty, and no knowledge of God in the land. Swearing, lying, and murder, and stealing and adultery break out; bloodshed follows bloodshed" (Hos 4:1–2). The opening chapter of Isaiah contains a sweeping indictment of covenant unfaithfulness: "Remove the evil of your doings from before my eyes; cease to do evil, learn to do good; seek justice, rescue the oppressed, defend the orphan, plead for the widow" (Isa 1:16–17). Mention of the orphan and the widow signal a concern for justice throughout all strata of society, especially for the marginalized without access to power. Amos summarizes the transgressions of Judah as "they have rejected the law of the LORD, and have not kept his statutes, but they have been led astray by the same lies after which their ancestors walked" (Amos 2:4b). Notably, Amos uses the word *pesha'*, translated here as "transgression," to characterize Judah's covenant unfaithfulness. In other contexts, *pesha'* means "rebellion," as in a vassal nation rebelling against an overlord by failing to obey the stipulations of the political treaty (see, for example, 2 Kgs 1:1; 8:20). Here, Amos accuses the people of an act of rebellion against God for failing to keep the terms of the covenant. By calling the people to remember and respect the covenant, the prophets functioned in what may be described as a conservative role. Ironically, in popular imagination, prophets are often depicted as liberals rather than conservatives. The prophets resist such categorizations; they are liberal in their call for economic justice (see below) even as they conserve the ancient tradition of the covenant.

Exclusive Loyalty to God

Faithfulness to the covenant is manifest first and foremost by worship of God alone. This may seem self-evident, but in a world where every culture worshiped multiple gods, loyalty to the God of Israel alone was more easily commanded than done. Influenced by their Canaanite neighbors, Israelites included Canaanite fertility gods in their worship rituals, evidenced by Isaiah's chastisement.

> You that burn with lust among the oaks, under every green tree; you that slaughter your children in the valleys, under the clefts of the rocks? Among the smooth stones of the valley is your portion; they, they, are your lot; to them you have poured out a drink offering, you have brought a grain offering. Shall I be appeased for these things? Upon a high and lofty mountain you have

set your bed, and there you went up to offer sacrifice. Behind the door and the doorpost you have set up your symbol [of a fertility god]; for, in deserting me, you have uncovered your bed, you have gone up to it, you have made it wide; and you have made a bargain for yourself with them, you have loved their bed, you have gazed on their nakedness. You journeyed to Molech [chief god of the Ammonites] with oil, and multiplied your perfumes; you sent your envoys far away, and sent down even to Sheol [the place of the dead]. (Isa 57:5–9)

Jeremiah uses graphic language to compare the people of Judah to a wild animal in heat. "How can you say, 'I am not defiled, I have not gone after the Baals [Canaanite gods]'? Look at your way in the valley; know what you have done—a restive young camel interlacing her tracks, a wild ass at home in the wilderness, in her heat sniffing the wind! Who can restrain her lust? None who seek her need weary themselves; in her month they will find her" (Jer 2:23–24). As we saw above, Hosea's life reflects what we may call "spiritual adultery" by the people of Israel. When he marries a prostitute, he is playing the part of God, bound by covenant to a people who continue to seek other partners. Micah likewise condemns Israel's harlotry: "All her images shall be beaten to pieces, all her wages shall be burned with fire, and all her idols I will lay waste; for as the wages of a prostitute she gathered them, and as the wages of a prostitute they shall again be used" (Mic 1:7). Images or idols were expressly forbidden in the laws given at Mt Sinai. Again, we turn to Isaiah where we find a parody of idol-making, poking fun at the person who cuts down a tree, fashions half of it into an idol, and uses the other half to fuel a fire. The punch line is, "No one considers, nor is there knowledge or discernment to say, 'Half of it I burned in the fire; I also baked bread on its coals, I roasted meat and have eaten. Now shall I make the rest of it an abomination? Shall I fall down before a block of wood?'" (Isa 44:19).

The prophets also criticize political leaders for turning to other nations in times of crisis, seen as a sign of disloyalty to God, as if God were not powerful enough to offer political protection against threatening nations. The familiar sign of Immanuel ("God with us") is given precisely in such a time. In 734 BCE, Syria and the northern kingdom of Israel agreed to wage war against the southern kingdom of Judah. "When the house of David heard that Aram [Syria] had allied itself with Ephraim [Israel], the heart of Ahaz [King of Judah] and the heart of his people shook as the trees of the forest shake before the wind" (Isa 7:2). The prophet Isaiah is sent by God to warn King Ahaz "If you do not stand firm in faith, you shall not stand at all" (Isa 7:9b). The sign of Immanuel is meant to reassure King Ahaz that God is in control of political forces: "For before the child knows how to refuse the evil and choose the good, the land before whose two kings you are in dread will be deserted" (Isa 7:16). Isaiah is called upon again some thirty-three years later when the Assyrian army is besieging Jerusalem and King Hezekiah wonders who will come to his rescue. The prophet announces, "Therefore thus says the LORD concerning the king of Assyria: He shall not come into this city, shoot an arrow there, come before it with a shield, or cast up a siege ramp against it. By the way that he came, by the same he shall return; he shall not come into this city, says the LORD. For I will defend this city to save it, for my own sake and for the sake of my servant David" (Isa 37:33–35). Without describing the historical circumstances, Hosea accuses Ephraim, another name for the northern kingdom, of seeking alliances with Egypt or Assyria in times of trouble: "For they have gone up to Assyria, a wild ass wandering alone; Ephraim has bargained for lovers" (Hos 8:9); "Ephraim has become like a dove, silly and without sense; they call upon Egypt, they go to Assyria" (Hos 7:11).

Economic Injustice

The Old Testament prophets are perhaps best known for their scathing critique of economic injustice. The writings of the eighth-century prophets, especially Amos and Micah, are especially harsh as they announce God's judgment on the rich and powerful. In the ancient agricultural economy of Israel and Judah, living at subsistence level was the norm as farmers and herders barely managed to support their families. In contrast, the rich live in luxury in their summer houses and winter houses (Amos 3:15). Amos depicts the conspicuous consumption of the rich, calling the women "cows of Bashan," an extremely fertile area in northern Israel: "Hear this word, you cows of Bashan who are on Mount Samaria, who oppress the poor, who crush the needy, who say to their husbands, 'Bring something to drink!'" (Amos 4:1). Surely, the scandal of women ordering men to serve them was not lost on the ancient audience. We can almost see these lazy women relaxing in chaise lounges on the sun porch calling for their men to bring them another martini! Of course, wives of the farmers and herders would have been pounding grain in the hot sun, hauling water from a distance, and tending to children. In another passage, Amos delivers a woe oracle, an announcement of death, to the idle rich. "Alas [woe] for those who lie on beds of ivory, and lounge on their couches, and eat lambs from the flock, and calves from the stall; who sing idle songs to the sound of the harp, and like David improvise on instruments of music; who drink wine from bowls, and anoint themselves with the finest oils, but are not grieved over the ruin of Joseph!" (Amos 6:4–6). These idle rich lounge around, eating meat from animals they didn't herd and can afford to slaughter, drinking wine fermented from grapes and rubbing their skin with oil from olives they didn't tend or harvest. Notice that grapes and olives are luxury crops, useful to these idle rich for wine and oil, but not the kind of crops a farmer needs to feed his family. So the more arable acreage the rich devote to grapes and olives, the less there is for staples like grain and vegetables. The sting of the indictment is in the final phrase of this woe oracle; the real sin of the rich is that they "are not grieved over the ruin of Joseph," that is, they don't care that their northern Israelite kin are suffering while they are reveling in luxury.

The prophet Micah joins Amos as they both rail against the injustice by which the leaders of the people exploit the poor: "Their hands are skilled to do evil; the official and the judge ask for a bribe, and the powerful dictate what they desire; thus they pervert justice" (Mic 7:3); "you who afflict the righteous, who take a bribe, and push aside the needy in the gate [the location of the ancient court system]" (Amos 5:12). The merchants use "wicked scales and a bag of dishonest weights" (Mic 6:11) to cheat the people. Amos recounts the conversation among dishonest merchants: "When will the new moon be over so that we may sell grain; and the Sabbath, so that we may offer wheat for sale? We will make the ephah [the quantity sold] small and the shekel [the price] great, and practice deceit with false balances, buying the poor for silver and the needy for a pair of sandals, and selling the sweepings of the wheat" (Amos 8:5–6). Rich landowners "covet fields, and seize them; houses, and take them away; they oppress householder and house, people and their inheritance" (Mic 2:2). The most vulnerable of society, the very ones supposed to be protected by the leaders, are exploited: "The women of my people you drive out from their pleasant houses; from their young children you take away my glory forever" (Mic 2:9). Micah's metaphor of cannibalism gruesomely denounces the actions of the rich against the poor: "you who hate the good and love the evil, who tear the skin off my people, and the flesh off their bones; who eat the flesh of my people, flay their skin off them, break their bones in pieces, and chop them up like meat in a kettle, like flesh in a caldron" (Mic 3:2–3).

I urge all readers at this point to put down this book and read through the books of the prophets Amos and Micah. On the one hand, the judgment announced to the rich for their exploitation and oppression of the poor assures us that God's justice will eventually prevail. On the other hand, by global standards, any of us reading this book are the rich; we are the ones being addressed by the divine voice.

Ritual without Righteousness

In past years, scholars routinely characterized the prophets as opponents of legalistic cultic ritual and proponents of spirit-enlivened relationships. With the clarity of hindsight, we realize that such statements served to further scholars' agendas more than they reflected the prophetic texts. Yes, the prophets criticized religious ritual—but in the context of righteousness. That is, the prophets denounce the performance of religious ritual without the accompanying righteous behavior in the community. Again, Amos and Micah provide rebukes that echo through the centuries.

> "With what shall I come before the LORD, and bow myself before God on high? Shall I come before him with burnt offerings, with calves a year old? Will the LORD be pleased with thousands of rams, with ten thousands of rivers of oil? Shall I give my firstborn for my transgression, the fruit of my body for the sin of my soul?" He has told you, O mortal, what is good; and what does the LORD require of you but to do justice, and to love kindness, and to walk humbly with your God? (Mic 6:6–8)

> I hate, I despise your festivals, and I take no delight in your solemn assemblies. Even though you offer me your burnt offerings and grain offerings, I will not accept them; and the offerings of well-being of your fatted animals I will not look upon. Take away from me the noise of your songs; I will not listen to the melody of your harps. But let justice roll down like waters, and righteousness like an ever-flowing stream. (Amos 5:21–24)

At first read, the prophets seem to be saying that God does not like their religious rituals and would rather they did not perform them. But how does that square with the laborious instructions in Exodus, Leviticus, and Deuteronomy, by which every detail of various religious rituals is painstakingly described? To simply say that God does not like religious ritual contradicts the voice of God in the rest of the Old Testament. In the context of the prophetic message, the issue is better stated that God does not like their religious rituals because they are not accompanied by righteous behavior in the community. God is not impressed with rituals in which the people are simply 'going through the motions.' Given a choice between righteous behavior and religious ritual, God would rather have righteous behavior. Offerings of justice and love within the community and offerings of love and humility to God are to be preferred any day over offerings of animals, grain, or oil.

Two centuries later, the prophet Jeremiah takes up the same issue. The concept of the Jerusalem Temple as the place where God has chosen to dwell with the people has become perverted into the place God must protect. The people have ascribed almost magical powers to the Jerusalem Temple, believing that God would not bring any harm to the structure or the people who perform the religious rituals there, no matter what. But Jeremiah brings a word of warning about this mindset in his so-called Temple Sermon.

> The word that came to Jeremiah from the LORD: Stand in the gate of the LORD's house, and proclaim there this word, and say, Hear the word of the LORD, all you people of Judah, you that enter these gates to worship the LORD. Thus says the LORD of hosts, the God of Israel: Amend your ways and your doings, and let me dwell with you in this place. Do not trust in these deceptive words: "This is the temple of the LORD, the temple of the LORD, the temple of the LORD." For if you truly amend your ways and your doings, if you truly act justly one with another, if you do not oppress the alien, the orphan,

and the widow, or shed innocent blood in this place, and
if you do not go after other gods to your own hurt, then I
will dwell with you in this place, in the land that I gave of
old to your ancestors forever and ever. (Jer 7:1–7)

Like his predecessors, Jeremiah counters the false belief that religious ritual guarantees God's presence in the Jerusalem Temple. Rather, the prophets contend that religious ritual without
righteousness is a waste of time (and resources). What God truly wants is justice and righteousness enabled and enhanced by
worship.

Hope of Ultimate Salvation by God's Grace and Mercy

The prophets were overcome by the divine spirit and called to
speak as the messenger of the divine. Many times their message criticized harshly the daily ethics of society. The prophets,
of all people, knew the failings of the people of ancient Israel.
Yet they also offer hope of salvation. Sometimes the hope is
couched in language of repentance and amendment of ways, as
in the Jeremiah quotation above. In that case, one could say that
the hope of salvation is deserved—if the people behave as they
should as people of the covenant, then they will see the salvation of God. But, surprisingly, sometimes the hope is couched
in terms of God's mercy alone. Even though the people have
done nothing deserving salvation, God decides to offer salvation
anyway to at least a remnant of the people. The prophet Hosea
gives us a glimpse into the divine heart, as God debates deserved
destruction versus undeserved salvation.

When Israel was a child, I loved him, and out of Egypt
I called my son. The more I called them, the more
they went from me; they kept sacrificing to the Baals
[Canaanite gods], and offering incense to idols. Yet it
was I who taught Ephraim [another name for Israel] to
walk, I took them up in my arms; but they did not know
that I healed them. I led them with cords of human kind

ness, with bands of love. I was to them like those who lift infants to their cheeks. I bent down to them and fed them. They shall return to the land of Egypt, and Assyria shall be their king, because they have refused to return to me. The sword rages in their cities, it consumes their oracle-priests, and devours because of their schemes. My people are bent on turning away from me. To the Most High they call, but he does not raise them up at all. How can I give you up, Ephraim? How can I hand you over, O Israel? How can I make you like Admah? How can I treat you like Zeboiim? [two cities destroyed along with Sodom and Gomorrah] My heart recoils within me; my compassion grows warm and tender. I will not execute my fierce anger; I will not again destroy Ephraim; for I am God and no mortal, the Holy One in your midst, and I will not come in wrath. (Hos 11:1-9)

Micah's final prophecy is hope that God's character traits of mercy and forgiveness will prevail, despite the sorry state of affairs at the moment. "Who is a God like you, pardoning iniquity and passing over the transgression of the remnant of your possession? He does not retain his anger forever, because he delights in showing clemency. He will again have compassion upon us; he will tread our iniquities under foot. You will cast all our sins into the depths of the sea. You will show faithfulness to Jacob and unswerving loyalty to Abraham, as you have sworn to our ancestors from the days of old" (Mic 7:18-20). Even Amos, the prophet of extreme judgment, ends with words of hope. "I will restore the fortunes of my people Israel, and they shall rebuild the ruined cities and inhabit them; they shall plant vineyards and drink their wine, and they shall make gardens and eat their fruit. I will plant them upon their land, and they shall never again be plucked up out of the land that I have given them, says the LORD your God" (Amos 9:14-15). Jonah summarizes the issue by reciting the ancient creed of Israel: "I knew that you are a gracious God and merciful, slow to anger, and abounding in steadfast love, and ready to relent from punishing" (Jonah 4:2b).

three

PRIEST

A KEY LEADERSHIP ROLE in ancient societies throughout the ancient Near East is the priest. As the one who has regular contact with the divine, the priest stands at the intersection of heaven and earth. In this chapter, we explore the vocation and duties of the priest.

Terminology

The most common Hebrew word for "priest" is *kohen*, a word from which many modern readers will recognize the derivative Jewish surname Cohen. The word *kohen* appears over 750 times in the Old Testament, in every book except Ruth, Daniel, and four of the Minor Prophets, a strong indication of the prominence of the priesthood in Old Testament thought. The grammatical form of the word is a Hebrew participle, the literal meaning of which is "one who performs a verbal action." In English, this type of noun often has the suffix *-er*; "one who sings" is a "singer" and "one who bakes" is a "baker." One well-known translation is the defiant question Cain asks God after slaying his brother Abel: "Am I my brother's keeper?" Here, the word "keeper" is a Hebrew participle, "one who keeps." This grammatical excursus is to point out, then, that we would normally expect our English translation of *kohen* to be "priester," that is, "one who priests." But language development often defies expectations. The English word "priest" actually derives from the Greek word *presbyteros*, "elder," presumably because the important role of "priester" was reserved for those with the wisdom of age. The Hebrew word *kohen* is routinely translated into *iereus* in the Greek version of the Old Testament, a word that comes over into English as the prefix "hier-", as in "hieroglyphics" (priestly-writings) and "hierarchy" (priestly-rule).

The Priestly Vocation

Whereas prophets report being overcome by an experience of the spirit of God and compelled to announce the word of God, the priests follow a more orderly route into divine service. In the ancient world, being a priest was a family affair, since heredity was the primary qualification. Typically, one was born into the priestly profession, so the biblical texts can refer to "the sons of Aaron" or "Levites" (meaning those born into the tribe of Levi). But priesthood was not an inalienable birthright, since inappropriate behavior could cause the disenfranchisement of priests. For example, fire consumed two sons of Aaron when "they offered unholy fire before the LORD, such as he had not commanded them" (Lev 10:1). The two sons of Eli, the priest at Shiloh, were condemned to death by God because "they treated the offerings of the LORD with contempt" (1 Sam 2:17). Likewise, the earth swallowed the Levite Korah and his family after he complained about the exalted status of Aaron with respect to the priesthood (Num 16:1–31). The story of Korah's contempt and punishment is interpreted as "a reminder to the Israelites that no outsider, who is not of the descendants of Aaron, shall approach to offer incense before the LORD" (Num 16:40a).

On the other hand, the story of the young Samuel demonstrates that boys from non-priestly families could be donated to the priesthood (1 Samuel 1). Although Samuel is never actually called a *kohen*, he performs all the duties of a *kohen*: offering sacrifices, divination, intercessory prayer, and anointing kings. Excavated texts give evidence that temples in the ancient Near East took in foundlings as a sort of social service agency. Perhaps some families donated their sons to the priesthood in gratitude to the deity or in dire economic circumstances. Similarly, we encounter a priest in Judges 17 who is called both "from the clan of Judah" and "a Levite" (Judg 17:7). The young man is employed as a personal priest at a house shrine in the hill country of Ephraim until the tribe of Dan makes him a better offer. He leaves Ephraim and travels with the tribe of Dan, which is migrating from the southwest coast to the northern Galilee. Apparently, the term Levite here is a vocational term and not a lineage per se.

Since priests were dedicated to full-time service to God, they relied on the people they served to support them economically. When the geographic territory of the Promised Land was apportioned by lot, the tribe of Levi was deliberately excluded from being assigned "an inheritance." Rather, they were assigned forty-eight towns and the surrounding pasture lands throughout the entire territory, so that each tribe gave up some villages and land to support the Levites. Once the centralization of worship and sacrifice took place in Jerusalem in the mid-seventh century BCE, the priests were supported by receiving a portion of the offerings brought by the people. The summary in Deut 18:3–4 is instructive: "This shall be the priests' due from the people, from those offering a sacrifice, whether an ox or a sheep: they shall give to the priest the shoulder, the two jowls, and the stomach. The first fruits of your grain, your wine, and your oil, as well as the first of the fleece of your sheep, you shall give him."

The practice of supporting religious personnel with offerings was widespread throughout the ancient Near East, known as far back as 2000 BCE. Thousands of texts excavated from southern Mesopotamia record the issuance of commodities to temple personnel as payments for services. Known as "prebends," these payments regularly included a share of the sacrificial offerings, as well as dates or barley, clothing or wool, shoes, blankets, and so forth. Since the required daily offerings to gods in Mesopotamia included staggering amounts of food items, temple personnel could always be assured of lots of "leftovers." One text, "Daily Sacrifices to the Gods of the City of Uruk," a city located on the Euphrates 100 miles north of Basra, Iraq, calls for 216 containers of beer, 243 loaves of bread, 50 rams, 3 bulls, plus quantities of dates, lambs, ducks, birds, and eggs. Another text from a temple in Nippur, 85 miles southeast of Baghdad, Iraq, lists on one side the bread and beer presented as offerings to the god Ninurta. On the other side are listed distributions to temple personnel, the total of which equals the total offerings from the first side, an ancient version of a balanced budget.

Not unexpectedly, abuses in the prebendary system could occur with some priests taking more than their share by deceit or force, so that others received less than their allotted prebends. The early chapters of 1 Samuel recount the fate of the sons of Eli, the kindly priest at Shiloh who reassured Hannah in her barrenness and was a father-figure to the boy Samuel. They are introduced in the narrative by saying, "Now the sons of Eli were scoundrels; they had no regard for the LORD or for the duties of the priests to the people" (1 Sam 2:12–13a), not the most auspicious beginning. Their behavior with respect to the offerings made at the Shiloh temple was despicable. "When anyone offered sacrifice, the priest's servant would come, while the meat was boiling, with a three-pronged fork in his hand, and he would thrust it into the pan, or kettle, or caldron, or pot; all that the fork brought up the priest would take for himself" (1 Sam 2:13b–14a). As if that wasn't bad enough, the sons of Eli ignored the strict sacrificial rituals specifying the burning of fat as a "pleasing odor to the LORD" (for example, Lev 3:5). These corrupt priests would demand meat from the offering before the fat was removed and burned. "And if the man said to him, 'Let them burn the fat first, and then take whatever you wish,' he would say, 'No, you must give it now; if not, I will take it by force'" (1 Sam 2:16). When the worshiper needs to remind the priest of the rubrics of the ritual, something is amiss. Today, our pastors, rabbis, and imams do not receive shoulders and stomachs of animals, but they are economically supported by the congregations they serve, since tithes and offerings go to pay their salaries.

Duties of the Priests

The priests of ancient Israel were ritual specialists set apart for religious service. Like modern pastors, rabbis, and imams, their authority came both from the divine and from the community. The ancient priests worked in the 'cultus' or 'cult,' the words scholars use to mean the formal religious life of ancient societies. In the ancient world, the word *cult* means the orthodox way of worshiping God. The English word derives from Latin roots where it means "care" or "adoration." These ancient roots can be seen in the word "cultivation," care of the soil in order to allow full usefulness. As individuals became more focused on the cultivation of a personal devotional relationship with God, the word apparently lost its moorings in authorized rituals and became associated with individual quests for spiritual experiences. This trajectory led to the unfortunate use of the word *cult* today to mean some crazy, off-the-wall, fanatical group controlled by a charismatic leader who brainwashes the members according to the leader's own personal revelations of divine will. That is, the word *cult* today means the exact opposite of what it meant in the ancient world.

In this section we will explore the duties of the priests in four broad arenas of ancient life in the cult. As you read, you will note the individualistic nature of worship in ancient Israel, a fact that comes as a surprise to most readers. Many think of ancient worship as just a more primitive version of what happens today on a Sunday morning (for Christians) or Friday evening (for Jews). Except for the three required annual festivals, ancient Israelites went to the temple and the priests for specific, individualized reasons: to offer sacrifices, to be purified, to seek the divine will, or to obtain a legal ruling. The distinct duties are drawn as a way of categorization; lived reality would have recognized a high degree of overlap among the categories.

Sacrifice

The word "sacrifice" today is divorced from its priestly heritage. Today, we think of lives 'sacrificed' in war, finding a measure of peace in the idea that a life so valued by family and friends was given up so that something greater could be achieved (peace, restraint of aggression, etc.). Baseball fans celebrate a 'sacrifice' fly, a ball hit to the outfield whereby the batter 'sacrifices' the opportunity to be on base for the greater benefit to the team of advancing the player already on base. The fundamental commonalities in these two examples is the loss of something valuable and the greater benefit achieved by the action. Both of these characteristics undergird the ancient practice of sacrifice in the Old Testament and throughout the ancient Near East. Valuable items, animals and agricultural produce in the case of ancient Israel, and perhaps sons in the case of other cultures, were given up by the worshiper for the greater benefit of the divine presence. How the sacrifice and the divine presence were related is never exactly explained in the Old Testament. We are left centuries later to ascribe motivations by observing actions and directions for rituals.

HIERARCHY OF VALUE OF SACRIFICES

Time after time, the instructions for sacrificial ritual list the acceptable offerings, beginning with the most valuable. If the offering is to be an animal, the most valuable was the male without blemish from the *baqar*, the general Hebrew word that designates large livestock like cattle or oxen (Lev 1:3). Such animals would have been used in agriculture as draught animals for plowing, hauling wagons, and so forth. For a sacrifice of well-being, either a male or female large animal is equally acceptable (Lev 3:1). If the large animal is not available, then the worshiper should bring a male without blemish from the *tso'n*, the general Hebrew word for small livestock like sheep and goats (Lev 1:10). Sheep and goats provided milk, wool, and goat hair for daily needs of the family. Again, for the sacrifice of well-being, female small animals are equally acceptable to males (Lev 3:6). If a worshiper cannot bring a sheep or goat, the next acceptable sacrifice is birds, either turtledoves or pigeons (Lev 1:14). A similar hierarchy exists for grain offerings, from the fine flour with oil and frankincense to the baked grain with oil (Lev 2:1, 4–7). Noteworthy is the accommodation for economic circumstances of the worshiper, implying that participation in the sacrificial experience is more important than the sacrificial victim. Of course, human nature being what it is, we can imagine the talk around the dinner table as families compared sacrificial values.

CIRCUMSTANCES OF SACRIFICE

Generally speaking, the texts presume that sacrifices are the normal way of being in relationship with God in ancient Israel. In the same way that God enters into the biblical narrative in Gen 1:1 without need of introduction, sacrifices occur without cogent explanation. Cain brings an offering from the field and Abel from the flock (Gen 4:3–4); Noah built an altar and sacrificed animals on it (Gen 9:20); the book of Leviticus opens, "When any of you bring an offering . . ." as if this is the way of life so expected that it need not be explained (Lev 1:3). We are generally left to guess at the underlying circumstances based on what the sacrifices are called in the texts. The 'whole burnt' sacrifices take their name from the Hebrew word *'olah*, from the verbal root that means "to go up." Since the entire animal is burned up on the altar and the smoke goes up into the sky, the "going up" sacrifice is aptly named. (Transliteration of the Hebrew word *'olah* into Greek and then into German led to the word "*holocaust*.") Interestingly, the ritual instructions for the whole burnt sacrifices never offer any clue as to why an ancient Israelite would do such a thing. The animals were burnt completely on the altar, benefiting neither the priest nor the worshiper in any practical way. Picture the full offering plates being brought to the front of the sanctuary on Sunday morning and set ablaze! Not a single dime goes to pay the pastor's salary, to pay the light bill, or to provide food for the hungry. We can suppose that the sheer delight of being in relationship with God resulted in this valuable, and completely impractical, ritual.

The 'sacrifices of well-being' take their name from the Hebrew word *shalom*, a word often translated "peace," but whose core meaning is "wholeness." For example, when a person repays a loan, she *shaloms* it, restoring the creditor to wholeness. We can assume the worshiper who brought a *shalom* sacrifice was expressing joy in the wholeness of life under God. With this sacrifice, only certain particular parts of the animals were burned up in smoke, typically the fat covering the inner organs and the kidneys (Lev 3:3–4). The rest of the animal was shared between the priest and the worshiper, enacting a covenant meal of wholeness.

Unintentional sins were the occasion of the 'sin' sacrifices, from the Hebrew verbal root that means to sin by missing the mark. Details are given for unintentional sins by the anointed priest (Lev 4:1–12), the whole congregation (Lev 4:13–21), the ruler (Lev 4:22–26), and the common people (Lev 4:27–35). Once the sin is made known to the offender, he brings the specified sacrifice, lays hands on it, slaughters it, uses some of the blood to daub the altar, and burns up the fat and kidneys. If the offender is the anointed priest, the whole congregation, or the ruler, the remainder of the animal is disposed of outside the holy precinct area. For offenses by common people, the animal may be consumed by the priest, but only if eaten within the holy precinct (Lev 6:24–30). We can understand substitutionary atonement at work in this ritual. Blood in the ancient world was already known to be the essential ingredient for life. Observation alone reveals that when human or animal loses its blood, it dies. Reason, therefore, announces that blood is life. The animal's loss of blood, and therefore life, substitutes for the offender's deserved punishment. It may be that sins by priests, the whole congregation, or the ruler were considered so grievous that the animal was thought to be too contaminated to eat.

'Guilt' sacrifices are related to specific sins, and always carry restitution in addition to the sacrificial requirements. For example, if someone deceives his neighbor by robbery, including finding something that was lost by a neighbor and not returning it, the penalty is restoration of the loss plus twenty percent compensation plus the sacrifice of a ram, whose fat and kidneys are burned and flesh eaten by the priest (Lev 6:1–7; 7:1–6).

DIVINE PRESENCE

In some parts of the ancient Near East, sacrifices were understood to appease an angry deity or to assimilate the power of the deity into the human worshiper. Neither of these understandings was primarily operative in ancient Israel. Rather, sacrifice serves as the divinely-mandated means to signal human commitment to repair and restore relationships. In ancient Israel, sacrifice gives up something of value to receive something of greater worth, the restoration of divine-human relationships and human-human relationships.

Purification

A fundamental assertion of ancient Israel is that God is holy. By that is meant that God is wholly other than anything else in all creation, set apart from any other person or thing. The core meaning of the Hebrew word *qadosh*, often translated "holy" in English, is "set apart for something sacred." In the ancient literature, *qadosh* does not carry the moral judgment sometimes meant in modern English, as in "holier-than-thou." By definition, God is holy and everything else is not. In order to have contact with God, therefore, items must be made holy.

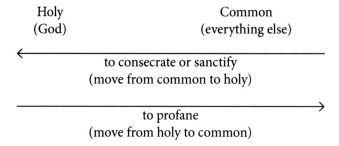

Holy   Common
(God)   (everything else)

← ————————————————————
to consecrate or sanctify
(move from common to holy)

———————————————————— →
to profane
(move from holy to common)

Rituals are provided that intentionally move items from common to holy, including people, places, time, and objects. The modern reader can relate to this concept by imagining an ordination service or a service of dedication of a church organ. Less familiar to modern readers is the process of profanation. In ancient Israel, items are disqualified from being in the holy category simply by contact with common things, even if unintentional. Note that this does not work the other way; simple contact with the holy does not move something from common to holy. The postexilic prophet Haggai succinctly summarizes the situation: "Thus says the LORD of hosts: Ask the priests for a ruling: If one carries consecrated meat in the fold of one's garment, and with the fold touches bread, or stew, or wine, or oil, or any kind of food, does it become holy? The priests answered, 'No'" (Hag 2:11–12). So, holiness cannot be 'caught' by one item from another, but commonness can 'infect' an item previously holy. Obviously, the priests were kept busy making sure that those things that should be holy—temple furniture, temple vessels, priests, vestments—stay holy, so that they can come in contact with God.

In a somewhat parallel fashion, categories existed in ancient Israel related to *clean* and *unclean*. Again, modern parlance is to be ignored in considering these terms; unclean has nothing to do with morally unsatisfactory. Rather, 'clean' means something like "in its proper category according to the way things are supposed to be." By contrast, 'unclean' means that something is outside of its proper category.

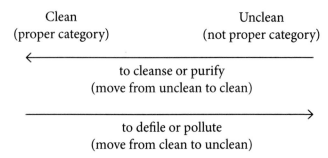

Clean   Unclean
(proper category)   (not proper category)

← ——————————————————————
to cleanse or purify
(move from unclean to clean)

——————————————————————→
to defile or pollute
(move from clean to unclean)

Again, in parallel fashion, the process of moving items from unclean to clean takes place by virtue of an intentional ritual. On the other hand, unintentional contact can cause an item to become unclean. We turn to the second half of Haggai's example: "Then Haggai said, 'If one who is unclean by contact with a dead body touches any of these, does it become unclean?' The priests answered, 'Yes, it becomes unclean'" (Hag 2:13). The rituals prescribed by Leviticus to cleanse or purify people or items usually involve appearing before the priests for a decision regarding the issue in question, a time of separation from the community, washing, and sacrifices. For example, Lev 14:1–32 discusses in detail the ritual cleansing of skin disease. The healed individual should go to the priest for examination and determination (vv. 1–3a). If the priest determines he is healed, two living birds and specific herbs should "be brought for the one who is cleansed," an implicit acknowledgement that such a person probably does not have sufficient resources even to offer two birds, the cheapest acceptable animal sacrifice (vv. 3b–4). One bird is killed and the other bird and herbs dipped into the first bird's blood. Then the blood is sprinkled on the individual seven times, the man is proclaimed clean, and the second bird is released into the open field (vv. 5–7). The man washes his clothes, shaves off his hair, and bathes (vv. 8–9). On the eighth day after the ritual, the healed individual offers a whole burnt offering consisting of two male lambs and one female lamb without blemish, or one male lamb and two turtledoves or pigeons if he cannot afford the three lambs, along with fine flour and oil. The blood from the sacrificed animals is daubed on his right ear, his right thumb, and his right big toe. Oil is poured into the priest's left palm, who uses his right forefinger to daub oil on the individual's right ear, right thumb, and right big toe; leftover oil is poured over the individual's head. Finally, the animals and grain are burned on the altar. The point is not that the details of this ritual are particularly worth remembering. Rather, the point is simply to highlight the explicit details and the care with which the ritual is to be carried out. From this, we get a sense of how important such issues were in the religious life of ancient Israel.

The most succinct job description for priests appears in Lev 10:10: "You are to distinguish between the holy [*qodesh*] and the common, and between the unclean and the clean" (see also Ezek 44:23). Obviously, keeping track of all the categories and rituals would keep the priests busy. This is really important work, because only an item classified as 'clean' is then eligible to be consecrated by ritual in order to come in contact with the Holy. That is, at no time may an unclean object come in contact with the Holy. This may seem like so much mind-numbing detail to modern readers, but the presence of the divine is at stake. Uncleanness would cause the divine Holy Other to leave the area. The Deuteronomist regularly asserts that the Lord will choose the place for the divine name to dwell (see, e.g., Deut 12:5; 14:23). Presumably, the flipside of this position is that the Lord can choose for the divine name to dwell somewhere else. The prophet Ezekiel shows us how this happens. In a vision, Ezekiel is carried to the gateway to the Jerusalem Temple and asked, "Mortal, do you see what they are doing, the great abominations that the house of Israel are committing here, to drive me far from my sanctuary?" (Ezek 8:6). After several more visions of the sinful actions of Israel's temple community, the glory of God left the Jerusalem temple by means of a wheeled throne decorated with cherubim (Ezek 10:18–19).

Divination

In the previous chapter, we explored the prophet's connection with the divine through the agency of the spirit. The priest, also, was understood to be connected with the divine will. But the priest's connection with the divine typically occurs through more tangible means, understood by the term "divination." Among ancient Israel's neighbors, the most common forms of divination were reading animal entrails, especially the position of the liver, and reading the flight formation of birds. Deuteronomy forbids forms of divination practiced in surrounding cultures: "No one shall be found among you who makes a son or daughter pass through fire, or who practices divination, or is a soothsayer, or an augur, or a sorcerer, or one who casts spells, or who consults ghosts or spirits, or who seeks oracles from the dead" (Deut 18:10–11). The author of these verses is keen to record a laundry list of forbidden magical actions. The Hebrew text uses different words for each of the items in the list, the exact meaning of which is now lost in the mists of history.

The first, "who practices divination," seems to be the general term defined more specifically by the following terms. The Hebrew uses a participle (see above) and then a plural noun of the root *qasam*, so the literal translation would be something like "one who divines divinings" or "a diviner of divinings," neither of which particularly helps us understand what is meant. Foreigners accused of doing this in the Old Testament include the elders of Moab and Midian (Num 22:7), the Philistines (1 Sam 6:2), a Canaanite woman (1 Sam 28:8), and the Ammonities (Ezek 21:28). The prophet Ezekiel describes the decision-making technique that will be used by the king of Babylon as he besieges Judah: "For the king of Babylon stands at the parting of the way, at the fork in the two roads, to use divination; he shakes the arrows, he consults the teraphim [figurines of household gods], he inspects the liver" (Ezek 21:21).

The next three in the laundry list of magical actions, "a soothsayer, or an augur, or a sorcerer," seem to be specific ways to discern the divine will. Some of us may not be able to articulate the exact meaning of these English words, so it will be no surprise that the Hebrew words are equally vague. The Hebrew word translated "soothsayer" uses the same three root letters as the normal Hebrew word for "cloud." The same root in Arabic indicates a natural sound, like the hum of insects or the whisper of leaves. Maybe the ancient "soothsayer" interpreted natural phenomena (cloud patterns? insect sounds? wind speeds?) to ascertain the divine will. The next term, "augur," is the translation of the Hebrew noun *nachesh*, probably related to the regular word for "serpent," *nachash*. Throughout the ancient world, snakes were understood to be crafty animals (see Gen 3:1), possessing supernatural powers. The term may have indicated originally that the person manipulated snakes or interpreted the markings of the serpentine movements left in the dust. Curiously, this term is used with respect to the cup that Joseph stashes in the luggage of his youngest brother Benjamin. "When they had gone only a short distance from the city, Joseph said to his steward, 'Go, follow after the men; and when you overtake them, say to them, "Why have you returned evil for good? Why have you stolen my silver cup? Is it not from this that my lord drinks? Does he not indeed use it for divination? You have done wrong in doing this"'" (Gen 44:4–5). Maybe here the term means something like "reading tea leaves." The third term, "sorcerer," is from the Hebrew word directly related to the Assyrian word that means witchcraft.

The final three descriptions of forbidden activities seem more familiar to the modern reader. "One who casts spells" is related to the Hebrew verb that means "to join together." In the priestly literature of Exodus, for example, the priests join together the curtains of the Tabernacle, the flaps of the tent, and the straps of the ephod that hangs over the shoulders of Aaron. Perhaps "the one who casts spells" tied knots in pieces of wool or rope in an effort to discern the divine will. The one who "consults ghosts or spirits" uses the Hebrew technical term that means "to inquire of the divine." One of the two nouns uses the same consonants as the word for "ancestor" and the second noun is from the Hebrew word for "knowledge." A reasonable interpretation would be something like a séance, in which a dead ancestor, who is well-known to the inquirer and who has access to secret knowledge, is entreated to communicate with the living. Finally, one "who seeks oracles from the dead" also uses a priestly technical term that means "to seek at the divine place." The prophet Isaiah points to the forbidden behavior: "Now if people say to you, 'Consult the ghosts and the familiar spirits that chirp and mutter; should not a people consult their gods, the dead on behalf of the living, for teaching and for instruction?' Surely, those who speak like this will have no dawn!" (Isa 8:19–20).

The acceptable means of divination in ancient Israel was casting lots, although the details are obscure. The Hebrew word for "lot" is *goral*, probably related to the Arabic word that means "stones" or "stony place." Scholars surmise, therefore, that lots were small stones with distinguishing features or marks, something like modern dice. The lots were set in motion, presumably by some sort of hand motion; Hebrew verbs associated with the noun for "lot" include falling down, going up, throwing, and hurling. When the lot came to rest, the resultant positioning or marks or both indicated the decision. A remnant of folk wisdom that survived the centuries claims, "The lot is cast into the lap, but the decision is the LORD's alone" (Prov 16:33).

As the Israelites were poised to enter the Promised Land, God instructed Moses on how to allocate the territory to the twelve tribes: "To a large tribe you shall give a large inheritance, and to a small tribe you shall give a small inheritance; every tribe shall be given its inheritance according to its enrollment. But the land shall be apportioned by lot; according to the names of their ancestral tribes they shall inherit. Their inheritance shall be apportioned according to lot between the larger and the smaller" (Num 26:54–56). The geographical boundaries for each tribe according to lot are spelled out in the Numbers 32 for the tribes settling to the east of the Jordan River and in the book of Joshua for the tribes settling to the west of the Jordan River (Joshua 14–19). One of the more familiar texts concerned with casting lots is the story of Jonah. We were reminded in Chapter 2 about his westward trek away from the word of the Lord by means of a ship launched from the port of Joppa. When the ship was endangered by a great storm, "The sailors said to one another, 'Come, let us cast lots, so that we may know on whose account this calamity has come upon us.' So they cast lots, and the lot fell on Jonah" (Jonah 1:7). Also familiar to most readers is the verse, "they divide my clothes among themselves, and for my clothing they cast lots" (Ps 22:18), reinterpreted in the Gospels as applying to the crucifixion of Jesus.

The book of Esther, in addition to celebrating the savvy actions of Queen Esther, explains how the casting of lots supplies the reason for a popular Jewish festival. Haman, the evil advisor to the king, receives permission to issue a royal edict of genocide against all Jews in the kingdom. "In the first month, which is the month of Nisan, in the twelfth year of King Ahasuerus, they cast Pur—which means 'the lot'—before Haman for the day and for the month, and the lot fell on the thirteenth day of the twelfth month, which is the month of Adar" (Esth 3:7). Notice that the term *pur*, probably an Assyrian loan word, is introduced by the author as a synonym for the normal Hebrew word *goral*, "lot," a point that will become important at the very end of the story. Esther, after satisfying her husband with food and drink, tells him about the evil edict and asks for relief for the Jews throughout the kingdom. The king grants her request, signing a new edict allowing the Jews to defend themselves against Haman's henchmen.

Moreover, the king orders Haman to be hanged on the very gallows Haman had built for his enemy. So, the story summarizes, "Haman son of Hammedatha the Agagite, the enemy of all the Jews, had plotted against the Jews to destroy them, and had cast Pur—that is 'the lot'—to crush and destroy them; but when Esther came before the king, he gave orders in writing that the wicked plot that he had devised against the Jews should come upon his own head, and that he and his sons should be hanged on the gallows. Therefore these days are called Purim, from the word Pur" (Esth 9:24–26a). Today, the festival is a boisterous celebration; as the story is read aloud, the audience blows noisemakers, rings bells, and makes catcalls at every mention of the name Haman.

The astute reader will have noticed that the examples of casting lots mentioned so far do not involve priests, so casting lots was not necessarily restricted to the priests. A specialized, priestly form of the general biblical use of lots may be the Urim and Thummim. The meanings of the words are uncertain, so they are typically just transliterated from the Hebrew words. They are described as part of the priestly vestments first used by Aaron in the wilderness: "In the breastpiece of judgment you shall put the Urim and the Thummim, and they shall be on Aaron's heart when he goes in before the LORD; thus Aaron shall bear the judgment of the Israelites on his heart before the LORD continually" (Exod 28:30; see also Lev 8:8). Apparently, they are small enough to fit inside the breastpiece and light enough for Aaron to wear continually. Like the more general casting of lots, the Urim and Thummim were used by a priest to discern the specific will of God.

One example of the use of these devices is in a complicated narrative about King Saul, his son Jonathan, and a battle with the Philistines. After a narrow Israelite victory over the Philistines, Jonathan eats some honey he finds in the forest. Other soldiers roundly criticize him for disobeying his father's order to abstain from food until nightfall. King Saul wants to pursue the battle into the evening, and the priest accompanying the army suggests consulting the Lord. When there is nothing but divine silence, King Saul realizes that some kind of sin is preventing discernment of God's will. "Then Saul said, 'O LORD God of Israel, why have you not answered your servant today? If this guilt is in me or in my son Jonathan, O LORD God of Israel, give Urim; but if this guilt is in your people Israel, give Thummim.' And Jonathan and Saul were indicated by the lot, but the people were cleared. Then Saul said, 'Cast the lot between me and my son Jonathan.' And Jonathan was taken" (1 Sam 14:41–42). [The English words "the lot" used twice in this quotation are only implied in Hebrew.] Another example involving King Saul indicates the divine silence, saying, "When Saul inquired of the LORD, the LORD did not answer him, not by dreams, or by Urim, or by prophets" (1 Sam 28:6). Finally, the priestly tribe of Levi is inextricably linked with the use of Urim and Thummim when Moses pronounces his farewell blessing on the tribes: "And of Levi he said: Give to Levi your Thummim, and your Urim to your loyal one, . . . they place incense before you, and whole burnt offerings on your altar" (Deut 33:8a, 10b).

The wilderness ritual for the Day of Atonement includes the casting of lots over goats. Here the biblical text uses the more generic Hebrew *goral* for "lot," even though Aaron is the one controlling them. "He [Aaron] shall take the two goats and set them before the LORD at the entrance of the tent of meeting; and Aaron shall cast lots on the two goats, one lot for the LORD and the other lot for Azazel. Aaron shall present the goat on which the lot fell for the LORD, and offer it as a sin offering; but the goat on which the lot fell for Azazel shall be presented alive before the LORD to make atonement over it, that it may be sent away into the wilderness to Azazel" (Lev 16:7–10). Azazel is understood to be some kind of demonic spirit whose evil influence will be purged from the community when the scapegoat carries away the community's sins into the wilderness.

Teaching the Law

As quoted above, a succinct job description for priests appears in Lev 10:10: "You are to distinguish between the holy [*qodesh*] and the common, and between the unclean and the clean." The next verse is particularly applicable to our description of priests as teachers of the Law: "and you are to teach the people of Israel all the statutes that the LORD has spoken to them through Moses" (Lev 10:11). Once we grasp the breadth of knowledge that the priests needed to administer the sacrificial systems and the purification/sanctification systems, we see how the priests were in the best position in ancient Israel to be the experts on interpreting "all the statutes" given by God. The Old Testament has many, many words for "law"—statutes, ordinances, commandments, testimonies, judgments, precepts. Psalm 119 employs 176 verses to celebrate God's law as fine gold, sweet honey, silver, the heart's delight, lamp and light, and salvation. The summative Hebrew word for God's gracious gift of instructions on how to live as covenant people of God is *torah*, often translated into English as Law (with a capital *L*). Closer to the ancient Israelite understanding would be Teaching about Life with God. The noun *torah* comes from the verbal root that means "to throw or to shoot [arrows]." The development to the meaning "to instruct" could be from the 'throwing' of lots (see above) and instructing based on the positioning of the lots. Or perhaps the meaning developed from 'throwing' the finger to point out a particular direction (as in Gen 46:28, the way to Goshen). At any rate, by the time of the Hebrew used in the Old Testament, its meaning as "show the way, instruct, teach" is clearly in view; another noun coming from the same verbal root is *moreh*, "teacher."

The priests were the divinely-instituted vehicles through which the desired, specific behaviors were taught and administered. Since ancient life with God was not compartmentalized into what we would call 'sacred' and 'secular,' the priests were in the best position to learn, interpret, and apply the Law in the lives of the people. We noted above in the section on Divination that the priestly Levites were inextricably linked with the Urim and the Thummim in the farewell blessing of Moses. In the same poetic blessing, the Levites are described as teachers of the Law: "They teach Jacob your ordinances, and Israel your law" (Deut 33:10a). Previously, the Deuteronomist tells us, "Moses wrote down this law, and gave it to the priests, the sons of Levi, who carried the ark of the covenant of the LORD" (Deut 31:9).

The historical narratives of the Old Testament support the assertion that the priests were the teachers of the Law throughout several centuries of monarchical rule. Even allowing for bias on the part of the authors, the narratives consistently demonstrate the role of the priests as teachers. A few examples will suffice to illustrate. King Asa (913–873 BCE) is presented by the Chronicler as a reformer in the southern kingdom of Judah shortly after the division of the land into two kingdoms after Solomon died. Asa's reformation included erasing pagan shrines, justified by the observation, "For a long time Israel was without the true God, and without a teaching priest, and without law" (2 Chr 15:3). His son, King Jehoshaphat of Judah (873–849 BCE) appointed five officials and eleven priests as his representatives. "They taught in Judah, having the book of the law of the LORD with them; they went around through all the cities of Judah and taught among the people" (2 Chr 17:9). After an ill-advised alliance with the northern kingdom, the Chronicler's narrative seeks to redeem Jehoshaphat as one who fears and relies on God. "Moreover in Jerusalem Jehoshaphat appointed certain Levites and priests and heads of families of Israel, to give judgment for the LORD and to decide disputed cases. They had their seat at Jerusalem . . . whenever a case comes to you from your kindred who live in their cities, concerning bloodshed, law or commandment, statutes or ordinances, then you shall instruct them, so that they may not incur guilt before the LORD and wrath may not come on you and your kindred. Do so, and you will not incur guilt" (2 Chr 19:8, 10). A little over a century later, the northern kingdom was incorporated into the Assyrian empire. The authors of the narrative preserved in 2 Kings attribute the historical event in 721 BCE to God's anger over the wickedness of the people. Assyrian records confirm that inhabitants of the northern territory of Israel were relocated to other lands, while people from other parts of the Assyrian empire were brought in as settlers to the territory now called Samaria. "So the king of Assyria was told, 'The nations that you have carried away and placed in the cities of Samaria do not know the law of the god of the land; therefore he has sent lions among them; they are killing them, because they do not know the law of the god of the land.' Then the king of Assyria commanded, 'Send there one of the priests whom you carried away from there; let him go and live there, and teach them the law of the god of the land'" (2 Kgs 17:26–27). Soon after the end of the northern kingdom, King Hezekiah of Judah (715–687 BCE) advocated reform, including re-establishment of the economic support of the priests. "He commanded the people who lived in Jerusalem to give the portion due to the priests and the Levites, so that they might devote themselves to the law of the LORD" (2 Chr 31:4). The great reformer, King Josiah of Judah (640–609 BCE), is credited with observing the greatest Passover feast ever. For our purposes, we note that his instructions were delivered to "the Levites who taught all Israel" (2 Chr 35:3). As a final example, we cite the actions of Ezra in the mid- to late-fifth century BCE. "They [the people gathered in Jerusalem] told the scribe Ezra to bring the book of the law of Moses, which the LORD had given to Israel. Accordingly, the priest Ezra brought the law before the assembly, both men and women and all who could hear with understanding." Ezra read from the book of the law all morning. With him in front of the people were some Levites. "So they [the Levites] read from the book, from the law of God, with interpretation. They gave the sense, so that the people understood the reading. And Nehemiah, who was the governor, and Ezra the priest and scribe, and the Levites who taught the people said to all the people, 'This day is holy to the LORD your God; do not mourn or weep.' For all the people wept when they heard the words of the law" (Neh 8:1b–2, 7b–8).

Reading through the Law codes in the Old Testament (Exodus 21–23; Leviticus; Deuteronomy 12–25), the reader is struck by the juxtaposition of laws governing worship festivals, incest, false weights, murder, idolatry, and so forth. All life is life in covenant relationship with God, so all of life is subject to God's desires, expressed in the Law. We should not think of the Law as negative, even though it certainly did function to constrain bad behavior. Rather, the Law was God's gracious instruction to God's chosen people about how to live in covenant relationship as "a priestly kingdom and a holy nation" (Exod 19:6). Many Christians have been taught to see the Old Testament Law (and Judaism) as legalistic, by which is meant a "works-righteousness" mindset. That is, many have been told that the ancient Israelites (and Jews) thought that the way to earn God's love was to keep the Law. But this is a pejorative Christian claim that is not supported by the Old Testament texts themselves. Rather, God loves the Israelite people, chooses them for a particular vocation in the world, and then expects them to live in ways that reflect the divine will.

Priests and Levites

We have seen that the priestly role is described by multiple terms in the Old Testament: "priests," "sons of Aaron," "Levites," "Levitical priests." As we turn to the question of the distinctiveness of these terms, we immediately confront the complexity of the textual history. The texts as we have them in the Old Testament came together over many years from many sources, with a very complicated literary history. To oversimplify the issue, the Priestly writers and compilers in the Babylonian Exile of the sixth century BCE trace their lineage to Aaron, so naturally they highlight Aaron's role as founder of the priesthood in the wilderness. The writers and compilers of Deuteronomy, by contrast, are likely Levitical priests who do not count Aaron as their founding father, so naturally they highlight the role of the Levites in the ancient history of Israel. Since the Priestly source in the Exile were the final editors, their work shapes the overall narrative so that we are left with the impression that the "sons of Aaron" priests performed the most sacred rituals, leaving the more mundane or routine tasks for the Levitical priests. But if we read carefully, traces of the struggle for priestly preeminence can be discerned in the texts.

The genealogy of Levi, the third son of Jacob and Leah, is traced through six generations in Exod 6:16–25. The description of the Tabernacle encampment in Numbers 3 sets apart the Levites for special priestly service with specific duties and designates the family head. The descendants of the firstborn of Levi, Gershon, are responsible for the tent and its curtains. The second son of Levi, Kohath, is listed as the father of four sons, the oldest of whom is the father of Aaron and Moses. Kohath's descendants are responsible for the Ark of the Covenant, the table, the lampstands, and other vessels. Levi's youngest son, Merari, fathers two sons, whose descendants are tasked with assembling and tracking the frames, bases, and cords for the tent.

The lineages as detailed in the texts highlight Aaron, since he is the only one whose descendants are reported into the sixth generation. Second in importance is Korah, the eldest son of the second son of Kohath, whose descendants are reported into the fifth generation. The genealogy ends, "These are the heads of the ancestral houses of the Levites by their families" (Exod 6:25b). The Priestly author of this section is clear about the pecking order.

> Then the LORD spoke to Moses, saying: Bring the tribe of Levi near, and set them before Aaron the priest, so that they may assist him. They shall perform duties for him and for the whole congregation in front of the tent of meeting, doing service at the tabernacle; they shall be in charge of all the furnishings of the tent of meeting, and attend to the duties for the Israelites as they do ser-

vice at the tabernacle. You shall give the Levites to Aaron and his descendants; they are unreservedly given to him from among the Israelites. But you shall make a register of Aaron and his descendants; it is they who shall attend to the priesthood, and any outsider who comes near shall be put to death. (Num 3:5–10)

Clearly, the author wants to use the term "Levites" to mean "those descended from Levi *other than through Aaron*." So even though Aaron is a Levite, meaning that his great-grandfather is Levi, in terms of priestly vocation, Aaron is not a Levite. So the Old Testament can speak about a category of priests known as "sons of Aaron" or simply "priests," and a category of priests known as "Levites" or "Levitical priests."

But what of the curious position of Moses in this genealogy? Other than being named as the younger brother of Aaron, Moses has no role whatsoever, including no mention of descendants. Remember, this genealogy is preserved by the priests who want to establish the preeminence of the Aaronic line. These priestly genealogies are the only places in the Old Testament where Aaron and Moses are linked as familial brothers. In the familiar story of Moses as the baby in the bulrushes, there is no indication at all of an older brother. Other places where the term "brother" is used to describe the relationship between Aaron and Moses, we could just as easily understand something like "partner" or "comrade." Kinship terms were often used in ancient Israel outside of blood kinship relationships.

Next we take note of the name Moses. The ending of the story of his miraculous rescue from the Nile explains, "She [the Pharaoh's daughter] named him Moses, 'because,' she said, 'I drew him out of the water'" (Exod 2:10b). The name depends on a word-play in Hebrew: His name is *Mosheh* because the verb for "draw out" is *mashah*. The fluent Hebrew speaker is supposed to overlook the fact that the grammatical form *mosheh* would mean "one who draws out" (that is, the Pharaoh's daughter) and not "one who is drawn out" (that is, the baby). Likewise, we are not supposed to be bothered by the fact that this is not the common, everyday verb for "remove from water" that everyone would know; in fact, this verb is used only one other place in the Old Testament. Scholars have documented the name Moses as an Egyptian name, meaning something like "begotten," for example in the Pharaoh's name Thutmoses (begotten of the god Thut) or Rameses (begotten of the god Ra). In the priestly genealogies, we note that the younger son of Merari, the youngest son of Levi, is named Mushi, a name derived from the same Hebrew root as the name Mosheh. Mushi is part of the family assigned to care for the tent frames, bases, and cords necessary for assembly of the Tabernacle. One possible explanation is that in retrospect, the prominence of Moses as leader of the Exodus–Wilderness–Sinai experience demanded a more impressive genealogy than simply being Mushi, son of Merari, son of Levi. So Mushi became Mosheh (Moses), familial brother of Aaron, the other revered leader.

Regardless of the identification of Mushi and Mosheh, we are left with two distinct priestly lineages, one that runs through Aaron and one that encompasses all the other Levites. The struggle for preeminence between descendants of Aaron (the Aaronites) and other descendants of Levi (sometimes called the Mushites) apparently lasted over several centuries and left traces in the biblical texts. Two categories of evidence may be marshaled. First, stories of conflict favor either the Aaronites or the Mushites. For example, the story of the Golden Calf lays the blame squarely at the feet of Aaron himself: "Aaron said to them, 'Take off the gold rings that are on the ears of your wives, your sons, and your daughters, and bring them to me.' So all the people took off the gold rings from their ears, and brought them to Aaron. He took the gold from them, formed it in a mold, and cast an image of a calf; and they said, 'These are your gods, O Israel, who brought you up out of the land of Egypt!'" (Exod 32:2–4). Moses summons the "sons of Levi" who circulate among the offenders with swords, killing "about three thousand." Moses said, "Today you have ordained yourselves for the service of the LORD, each one at the cost of a son or a brother, and so have brought a blessing on yourselves this day" (Exod 32:29). In another story, two sons of Aaron, Nadab and Abihu, "offered unholy fire before the LORD" and were devoured by divine fire themselves (Lev 10:1–2). On the other hand, Phinehas, grandson of Aaron, is the hero when he spears an Israelite man engaging in sexual relations with a Midianite woman. As a result, God instructs Moses: "Therefore say, 'I hereby grant him my covenant of peace. It shall be for him and for his descendants after him a covenant of perpetual priesthood, because he was zealous for his God, and made atonement for the Israelites'" (Num 25:12–13).

During David's reign, two chief priests were appointed, one from each of the lineages we have been discussing. The Mushite or Levitical lineage was represented by Abiathar, a priest associated with the shrine of Shiloh, where the Ark of the Covenant was housed before David captured Jerusalem. The Aaronite lineage was represented by Zadok, a priest traced by the Chronicler to eight generations after Phinehas (1 Chr 6:4–8). Perhaps David's political acumen persuaded him to share priestly power rather than choose one lineage over another. In the struggle for succession in David's old age, the sides were clearly drawn. David's eldest living son Adonijah garnered support from Abiathar, the Levitical priest, and Joab, the commander of the army. David's son Solomon drew support from Zadok, the Aaronite priest, the prophet Nathan, and the commander of some foreign mercenaries and David's bodyguard (1 Kgs 2:7–8). After Solomon was anointed, "The king said to the priest Abiathar, 'Go to Anathoth, to your estate; for you deserve death. But I will not at this time put you to death, because you carried the ark of the Lord GOD before my father David, and because you shared in all the hardships my father endured.' So Solomon banished Abiathar from being priest to the LORD, thus fulfilling the word of the LORD that he had spoken concerning the house of Eli in Shiloh" (1 Kgs 2:26–27). Knowledgeable readers will recognize Anathoth as the place from which the prophet Jeremiah hails, probably establishing Levitical credentials for him.

When the united monarchy split into Israel and Judah under Solomon's son, King Rehoboam, King Jeroboam I of the northern kingdom established two temples. The one at Dan, the northern limit of the territory, was attended by Levitical priests; recall the story of the Levite priest migrating with the tribe of Dan from the coastal area to the northern Galilee in Judges 17. The temple at Bethel, the southern territorial limit, was attended by Aaronite priests, a tradition attested to in Judges 20 when the divine will is sought at Bethel under the priestly direction of Phinehas (yes, the same Phinehas).

Some texts indicate that the Levitical priests continued to hold sway in the northern parts of Israel until its fall in 721 BCE and may have brought their ancestral traditions south to Jerusalem as refugees from the Assyrians, traditions that were taken up by the Deuteronomist.

By the time the official position of "chief priest" developed at the Jerusalem temple, the descendants of Zadok of the line of Aaron were in full control of the priesthood. The centrality of Aaronite ancestry was so ingrained that war could break out when a non-Zadokite was installed as high priest, as happened in the centuries immediately before the turn of the era. The transliteration of the Hebrew word Zadokites yields the Greek word Sadducees, the Jewish sect most concerned with priestly ritual in the New Testament, even if accommodation to the Roman overlords is the price to be paid.

four

SAGE

IN THIS CHAPTER WE explore the leadership role of the sage, the wise one who served as advisor in the family and in the royal court. The sage is the least-institutionalized of the leadership roles under consideration, leaving fewer traces in the biblical records.

Terminology

In English, the word 'sage' means a person distinguished for his or her wisdom (in addition to meaning an herb and a color). Unlike what we have seen with the preceding three leadership roles in the Old Testament, Hebrew has multiple words to describe the leadership role of 'sage.' Most often, the sages are simply called "the wise," using a form of the Hebrew word *chakam*. Often, the sages are referred to as "elders," from the Hebrew verb *zaqen*, the literal meaning of which is "to be old." In Old Testament thought, wisdom accompanied old age, so that those in the community who were seniors were respected for their accumulated years of wisdom. Sometimes the sages are called "counselors," using a form of the Hebrew verb *ya'ats*, presumably deriving from their importance in giving counsel to others. Sometimes they are described as having "understanding" or "discernment," using a form of the Hebrew root *biyn*.

The Role of the Sage in Society

In this section we explore two major societal locations for the sage in the ancient Near East, the family and the royal court. Then we turn to evidence of the role of sages in foreign kingdoms and examine post-Old Testament traditions.

Family and Tribal Life

The first eight books of the Old Testament, Genesis through Ruth, paint a picture of life centered on family and tribe. We remind the reader yet again of the complex compositional history of the Old Testament, written and edited by multiple sources over a considerable period of time. Whether the biblical picture of family and tribal life is accurate in all its details is beside the point for this discussion. Rather, we are interested in the way the biblical narratives *present* family and tribal life, as a first step in discerning a trajectory of the leadership role of the sage. According to the texts, multiple generations live together in small villages, providing for each other's needs for food and shelter. When the family is threatened, the extended family network of the clan or the tribe provides assistance. When tribes are threatened, a charismatic leader arises to rally the necessary resources to counter the threat. Once resolved, the people return to their nomadic and agricultural ways of life. Patriarchs are in charge of their family units, invested with the authority to make decisions on behalf of the extended family.

A logical next step is the appointment of those who will be in charge of decisions for clans or tribes, a patriarch of the patriarchs, so to speak. Especially as the families and tribes move from a nomadic lifestyle to agricultural settlements, the need arises for leaders who will adjudicate disputes between clans and tribes. These are the ones the Old Testament narratives label as "elders," selected for the wisdom and experience garnered from years of life. The phrase, "elders of Israel" is first used in Exod 3:16, when God instructs Moses through the voice in the burning bush, "Go and assemble the elders of Israel, and say to them, 'The LORD, the God of your ancestors, the God of Abraham, of Isaac, and of Jacob, has appeared to me, saying: I have given heed to you and to what has been done to you in Egypt." There is no explanation of who these elders are nor their leadership role in society. We are left to find clues elsewhere. The book of Deuteronomy, set as the farewell speech of Moses as the people as poised to enter the Promised Land, yields information about the role of the elders in ancient Israelite society.

Moses begins his speech by recalling words from God to leave the mountain of revelation and head for the land promised to their ancestors. The first episode in the wilderness Moses recalls is his complaint that the burden of leadership was too much for him to bear. So God instructed him to "choose for each of your tribes individuals who are wise, discerning, and reputable to be your leaders" (Deut 1:13). After assent from the people, Moses "took the leaders of your tribes, wise and reputable individuals, and installed them as leaders over you" (Deut 1:15a). This episode is initially reported in Exodus 18, with two important differences. First, Jethro, the Midianite priest who is Moses' father-in-law, is the one who suggests this solution to the problem in Exodus; Jethro is not mentioned at all in the recollection in Deuteronomy. Second, in the Exodus account, Moses chooses "able" men. The Hebrew says they were men of *chayil*, a word that can mean "army, strength, power, or might." Curiously, the Deuteronomic version does not use this word, even though the chosen leaders are installed as "commanders of thousands, commanders of hundreds, commanders of fifties, commanders of tens, and officials, throughout your tribes" (Deut 1:15b), deliberately invoking military imagery. Rather, the men are chosen as leaders because they are "wise" (*chakam*). Their assigned duties involve adjudicating disputes: "Give the members of your community a fair hearing, and judge rightly between one person and another, whether citizen or resident alien" (Deut 1:16). Moses himself will serve as the court of appeal. Later in Deuteronomy, these individuals who function as community judges are called "elders." For example, if a son will not obey either of his parents, even after repeated discipline, "then his father and his mother shall take hold of him and bring him out to the elders of his town at the gate of that place" (Deut 21:19). The elders hear the witness of the parents and pronounce judgment (in this case, death by stoning). Or if a husband accuses his wife of not being a virgin on their wedding night, "the father of the young woman and her mother shall then submit the evidence of the young woman's virginity to the elders of the city at the gate" (Deut 22:15). Upon examination, the elders adjudicate the dispute and punish either the husband (whipping, a fine, and perpetual marriage to the wife) or the wife (death by stoning). Recall that in the final chapter of Ruth, Boaz solemnizes his right to redeem the property belonging to Ruth's father-in-law by going to the city gate and summoning ten elders of the city as legal witnesses (Ruth 4:1–12). Clearly, elders were involved in adjudicating legal matters in the early days of ancient Israel.

Other texts indicate elders as something other than local judges. One of the laws in Deuteronomy specifies what to do if someone is found murdered in the open countryside and no one knows who did it. "Then your elders and your judges shall come out to measure the distances to the towns that are near the body" (Deut 21:2). Once the determination is made as to which town is nearest to the murdered person, the elders of that town should perform a ritual to purge the town of any blood guilt (Deut 21:3–9). In this passage, the elders are specifically mentioned as a group of people separate from the judges; in fact, in verse 5 the Levites are said to be the ones who settle every dispute. The elders seem to be more like priests, breaking the neck of an unworked heifer in a valley with running water, washing their hands over the heifer's corpse, and praying for the forgiveness of any blood guilt.

In an episode recounted in 1 Samuel 11, the elders of the city of Jabesh negotiate peace terms with the Ammonites who are besieging their town (1 Sam 11:1–4). When Samuel goes to Bethlehem to carry out the divine instruction to anoint a king from among the sons of Jesse, "the elders of the city came to meet him trembling, and said, 'Do you come peaceably?'" (1 Sam 16:4b). In these two texts, the elders function like diplomats, representing their city against hostile (or potentially hostile) intruders. Likewise, in the wilderness episode involving Israel camped in the territory belonging to Moab, we read that the fear of the Israelites caused King Balak of Moab to send messengers to Balaam, a Mesopotamian seer (Num 22:5). Two verses later, "So the elders of Moab and the elders of Midian departed with the fees for divination in their hand; and they came to Balaam, and gave him Balak's message" (Num 22:7). The elders seem to be the ancient version of diplomatic couriers, presumably trusted by the king to deliver the message accurately and to negotiate a fair price. Finally, we note that two lists in Joshua discriminate between elders and other types of leaders: "All Israel, alien as well as citizen, with their elders and officers and their judges, stood on opposite sides of the ark" (Josh 8:33a); "Joshua summoned all Israel, their elders and heads, their judges and officers" (Josh 23:2a).

Life under the Monarchy

The presence of wise leaders to advise the king seems a natural development from wise leaders among the extended families and tribes. Inasmuch as elders were useful in resolving local disputes and representing their towns diplomatically, the monarchy found such persons to be useful in its role of governing the kingdom. Especially in the early days of the monarchy, when the tribal allegiances were still particularly strong, elders could profitably serve as liaisons between the king's administration and the tribal families.

In the account of why the northern tribes separated from the southern tribes after the death of Solomon, the role of the elders is prominent. Solomon's son Rehoboam was crowned king upon the death of his father. The northern tribes petitioned the new king: "Your father made our yoke heavy. Now therefore lighten the hard service of your father and his heavy yoke that he placed on us, and we will serve you" (1 Kgs 12:4). Presumably, the people were complaining about the forced labor and heavy taxes that Solomon had imposed on the kingdom. The narrative in 1 Kings 4–7 depicts this "heavy yoke," even if exaggerated: a conscripted labor force of over 180,000 men; provisions of food to support all those at the royal court, as well as 40,000 horses and 12,000 horsemen; provisions of food for 22,000 people as payment for the cedar needed for the temple and palace. Upon hearing the complaint of the northern tribes, King Rehoboam asks for three days to consider the matter. "Then King Rehoboam took counsel with the older men who had attended his father Solomon while he was still alive, saying, 'How do you advise me to answer this people?'" (1 Kgs 12:6). In this verse, we note three important matters. First, the ones consulted for advice were the "older men," the same Hebrew word translated elsewhere as "elders." Second, these elders had been prominent in the reign of Solomon. The Hebrew literally says, "the elders who were standing before Solomon, his father." Whether they were at the royal court by virtue of a leadership role in a tribe or by virtue of age alone, we cannot say. But, since Solomon created administrative districts that were deliberately not configured like the tribal lands, it is unlikely that tribal leaders would have had such a prominent role at the court. The more likely scenario is that the men were chosen for their wisdom, accumulated through years of experience, and for their political savvy (another form of wisdom). Third, the Hebrew root *ya'ats*, mentioned above in the 'Terminology' section, is used twice in this verse. The verb is used for both sides of the conversation: those who are giving *ya'ats* are advising or counseling; those who are receiving *ya'ats* are consulting or being advised. In this verse, Rehoboam "took counsel" (*ya'ats*) with the elders to ask them what they advise (*ya'ats*). The double use of the same verb highlights the important role of these elders in the royal court. The elders reply, "If you will be a servant to this people today and serve them, and speak good words to them when you answer them, then they will be your servants forever" (1 Kgs 12:7). Sage advice indeed! The elders recognize the pivotal nature of this moment in King Rehoboam's reign: Answer wisely, and the political crisis will be averted; answer foolishly, and disaster is at hand. When we hear the advice given by the elders, we can understand why the monarchy used wise sages as counselors. Unfortunately, King Rehoboam "disregarded the advice (*ya'ats*) that the older men gave (*ya'ats*) him, and consulted (*ya'ats*) with the young men who had grown up with him and now attended him" (1 Kgs 12:8). In Hebrew, the root *ya'ats* is annoyingly repetitive, driving home the point. The young men, in direct contradiction to the advice of the elders, advise Rehoboam to make the burden on the people even heavier than in the time of Solomon. The northern tribes return after three days to hear the king's answer to their complaint. "The king answered the people harshly. He disregarded the advice that the older men had given him and spoke to them according to the advice of the young men, 'My father made your yoke heavy, but I will add to your yoke; my father disciplined you with whips, but I will discipline you with scorpions'" (1 Kgs 12:13–14). Again, the narrator wants to drive home the point that the king ignored the wisdom of the sages. The northern tribes rejected the kingship of Rehoboam; "so Israel has been in rebellion against the house of David to this day" (1 Kgs 12:19). Looking past the tendentious nature of the narrative, designed to explain the division of the united monarchy after Solomon, we see the prominent role given to elders as counselors to the king.

Next we consider a text from the book of Ezekiel, prophecies relating to the destruction of Jerusalem in 587 BCE and the subsequent exile of the people to Babylon. In chapter 7, the prophet is announcing the approaching wrath of God for all the abominations committed by the people. Ezekiel paints a picture of the people becoming more and more desperate to escape the punishment, but the people's leaders are unable to perform their appointed roles. "Disaster comes upon disaster, rumor follows rumor; they shall keep seeking a vision from the prophet; instruction shall perish from the priest, and counsel from the elders. The king shall mourn, the prince shall be wrapped in despair, and the hands of the people of the land shall tremble" (Ezek 7:26–27a). The text highlights the four leadership roles at the time of the exile: the prophet, the priest, the elders, and the monarchy. Note that the elders are sought after for "counsel" (root *ya'ats*).

The book of Lamentations records poetic cries of despair over the destruction of Jerusalem, and especially the temple, by the Babylonians. Chapter 4 begins, "How the gold has grown dim, how the pure gold is changed! The sacred stones lie scattered at the head of every street" (Lam 4:1). Attributing the destruction to the justified wrath of God, the poet delineates the sins of the kingdom's leadership. "It was for the sins of her prophets and the iniquities of her priests, who shed the blood of the righteous in the midst of her . . . The LORD himself has scattered them, he will regard them no more; no honor was shown to the priests, no favor to the elders" (Lam 4:13, 16). Again, we see the elders as a specified group of leaders, alongside the prophets and the priests. Presumably, they did not give wise counsel to the king, since the destruction of Jerusalem was precipitated by royal rebellion against the Babylonian overlords.

In the section of the book of Isaiah known as Second Isaiah (Isaiah 40–55), we find an interesting reference to a "counselor," one who gives counsel or advice. Scholars attribute the texts in Second Isaiah to a prophetic voice in Babylon near the end of the exilic period (c. 540 BCE), whose mission is to encourage the exiles to return home and live again as God's covenant people. The opening verses of Isaiah 40 announce that Judah's punishment has ended and that God will now lead the people home in a Second Exodus. The poet then buttresses his announcement by describing the incomparable nature of God as Creator, as if to say, "if God can create the universe, creating a way to bring God's people back to Jerusalem is no big deal." Within this poem are two verses that point to the role of the sage in ancient Israel. "Who has directed the spirit of the LORD, or as his counselor has instructed him? Whom did he consult for his enlightenment, and who taught him the path of justice? Who taught him knowledge, and showed him the way of understanding?" (Isa 40:13–14). Of course, the answer to the rhetorical questions is 'no one.' We note the assumption, however, that there is such a role in society, someone who acts as a counselor to instruct and teach and enlighten. Here the prophet depends on the cultural understanding of God as King (see Chapter 1). Even as the earthly king has a wise counselor, one would expect that God has an attendant sage. In the rhetoric of the poem, the sage is not needed by God, but that does not negate the underlying assumption that every king needs a sage.

The sage as the attendant of the Divine King may underlie the imagery known as Lady Wisdom in Proverbs 8. Present with the Creator (Prov 8:22–31), the Sage is active in the rule of the monarchy. She asserts, "I have good advice and sound wisdom; I have insight, I have strength. By me kings reign, and rulers decree what is just; by me rulers rule, and nobles, all who govern rightly" (Prov 8:14–16).

Foreign Kingdoms

As a corollary to the position of the sage as an advisor in the Israelite monarchy, we turn to information gleaned about the role of the sage in foreign kingdoms. Inasmuch as Israel lived among foreign kingdoms, at times governed by them, and always located at the trade crossroads of Africa and Asia, patterns of leadership in foreign kingdoms must have influenced Israel. The Hebrew root *chakam*, "wise" is used in the vast majority of these references. In a prophecy of judgment on Babylon the prophet Jeremiah announces, "A sword against the Chaldeans, says the LORD, and against the inhabitants of Babylon, and against her officials and her sages!" (Jer 50:35). Later in the same prophecy, God warns, "I will make her officials and her sages drunk, also her governors, her deputies, and her warriors; they shall sleep a perpetual sleep and never wake, says the King, whose name is the LORD of hosts" (Jer 51:57). In a prophecy against Egypt, the prophet Isaiah taunts, "The princes of Zoan are utterly foolish; the wise counselors of Pharaoh give stupid counsel" (Isa 19:11a). Early in the book of Esther, the Persian king becomes enraged when his queen refuses to appear before him as he had commanded. "Then the king consulted the sages who knew the laws (for this was the king's procedure toward all who were versed in law and custom . . .)" (Esth 1:13) in order to decide what to do. Later in the same book, we find out that Haman, the king's right hand man and the antagonist of the story, also has sages at his disposal (Esth 6:13). So, we see that sages were a regular part of the royal court.

In several Old Testament texts, the phrase "wise men" seems to refer to foreigners who have a special kind of wisdom we might broadly label as 'magic.' Two well-known texts involve "wise men" in the art of dream interpretation. When Joseph is languishing in prison in Egypt, Pharaoh has a disturbing dream. "In the morning his spirit was troubled; so he sent and called for all the magicians of Egypt and all its wise men. Pharaoh told them his dreams, but there was no one who could interpret them to Pharaoh" (Gen 41:8). According to the narrative in the book of Daniel, King Nebuchadnezzar had virtually the same experience; no one was able to interpret his dream. "Because of this the king flew into a violent rage and commanded that all the wise men of

Babylon be destroyed" (Dan 2:12). When Daniel and his companions are about to be swept up into the royal pogrom, Daniel asks to be allowed to interpret the dream. When the king scoffs at his request, "Daniel answered the king, 'No wise men, enchanters, magicians, or diviners can show to the king the mystery that the king is asking," (Dan 2:27), only God alone. Several years later, King Belshazzar trembles as a hand writes on the wall during a royal banquet. "The king cried aloud to bring in the enchanters, the Chaldeans, and the diviners; and the king said to the wise men of Babylon, 'Whoever can read this writing and tell me its interpretation shall be clothed in purple, have a chain of gold around his neck, and rank third in the kingdom.' Then all the king's wise men came in, but they could not read the writing or tell the king the interpretation" (Dan 5:7–8). Once again, Daniel is able to do what no one else can do.

"Wise men" who seem to be similar to magicians show up again in Pharaoh's court, this time in the context of the Israelites in slavery. In an effort to prove the power of their God, Moses and Aaron appear before Pharaoh, thrown down a staff and watch it change into a snake. "Then Pharaoh summoned the wise men and the sorcerers; and they also, the magicians of Egypt, did the same by their secret arts" (Exod 7:11). Later in the narrative, only the 'magicians' are mentioned as replicating the signs wrought by Moses and Aaron. This kind of 'magical wisdom' is evident in texts excavated from ancient Mesopotamia, texts in which 'wise men' consult various omens to discern the will of the gods. This particular nuance of the phrase 'wise men' may be what is meant when "wise men from the East" come to Jerusalem as a result of following a star (Matt 2:1–2). In ancient Israel, discerning the will of God is one of the duties of the priests (see Chapter 3).

Post-Old Testament Texts

The book of the Wisdom of Jesus the Son of Sirach, also known as Ecclesiasticus, was written in approximately 180 BCE. The author likely was the head of some kind of academy in Jerusalem and undertook to write down the accumulated wisdom he was teaching. Scholars understand the book of Sirach as a transitional link between the Wisdom Literature of the Old Testament and the rabbinic books that developed in Judaism after the destruction of the Second Temple in 70 CE. For Protestants, Sirach is part of the collection of books known as the Apocrypha; for Roman Catholics, these books are part of the canon of Scripture. In chapter 24, Lady Wisdom asserts that she was present at Creation and played a crucial role in Israel, similar to Proverbs 8. Beginning in chapter 38, the author contrasts various occupations with that of the scribe, asserting, "The wisdom of the scribe depends on the opportunity of leisure" (Sir 38:24a). The author then catalogues occupations too busy to become wise: farmers, artisans, seal makers, smiths, and potters. In the previous chapter he has extolled the work of physicians and pharmacists. Then he comes to his point: "All these rely on their hands, and all are skillful in their own work. Without them no city can be inhabited, and wherever they live, they will not go hungry. Yet they are not sought out for the council of the people, nor do they attain eminence in the public assembly. They do not sit in the judge's seat, nor do they understand the decisions of the courts; they cannot expound discipline or judgment, and they are not found among the rulers" (Sir 38:31–33). The one identified as the scribe seems to fill the role of the sage in the Old Testament: giving counsel, resolving local disputes, and advising rulers. Later in the same book, the author lists those men in the past who were leaders of society, including rulers, sages, and prophets, among others:

> There were those who ruled in their kingdoms,
>   and made a name for themselves by their valor;
> those who gave counsel because they were intelligent;
>   those who spoke in prophetic oracles;
> those who led the people by their counsels
>   and by their knowledge of the people's lore;

they were wise in their words of instruction;
those who composed musical tunes,
or put verses in writing;
rich men endowed with resources,
living peacefully in their homes—
all these were honored in their generations,
and were the pride of their times. (Sir 44:3–7)

In the Gospel of Matthew, the scribes and Pharisees receive harsh words in a series of seven woes. In the final woe section, we read, "Therefore I send you prophets, sages, and scribes . . ." (Matt 23:34a), an indication of the leadership role of sages even into the first century CE. In the first letter to the Corinthians, Paul contrasts God's wisdom with human wisdom. He says, "Where is the one who is wise? Where is the scribe? Where is the debater of this age? Has not God made foolish the wisdom of the world?" (1 Cor 1:20). The translation "one who is wise" is the sage.

Sage as Teacher

Only a small step needs to be taken to move from sage as wise counselor to sage as teacher. Obviously, one's own wisdom is a reliable basis on which to become a teacher of others, communicating the accumulated wisdom of life experiences as well as acquired knowledge.

Royal Court

In the Old Testament, the book of Proverbs is the collection *par excellence* of wise teachings. The superscription of the collection attributes the wise sayings that follow to "Solomon son of David, king of Israel," a continuation of the tradition of wisdom that accrued to Solomon over time. The opening verses set the tone for what follows, succinctly describing the purpose of the collection, what we would call today "educational outcomes": "For learning about wisdom and instruction, for understanding words of insight, for gaining instruction in wise dealing, righteousness, justice, and equity; to teach shrewdness to the simple, knowledge and prudence to the young" (Prov 1:2-4). The triad "righteousness, justice, and equity" particularly point to the royal court, showing the importance of wise counselors to the monarchy. The proverbs collected in chapters 10–21 are also specifically attributed to King Solomon. A later superscription also records Solomon's influence: "These are other proverbs of Solomon that the officials of King Hezekiah of Judah copied" (Prov 25:1). At the beginning of the final chapter of Proverbs, the sayings are attributed to King Lemuel, an otherwise unidentified king.

We may imagine a kind of royal school, in which wise sayings were preserved in writing and where young princes and aspiring officials were trained in the art of governing by sages. Read through the lens of royal training, many of the proverbs in these royal collections offer sage advice to a monarchy:

> Where there is no guidance, a nation falls,
>> but in an abundance of counselors there is safety.
> (Prov 11:14)

> The glory of a king is a multitude of people;
>> without people a prince is ruined. (Prov 14:28)

> Without counsel, plans go wrong,
>> but with many advisers they succeed. (Prov 15:22)

> A wise king winnows the wicked,
>> and drives the wheel over them . . .
> Loyalty and faithfulness preserve the king,
>> and his throne is upheld by righteousness. (Prov 20:26, 28)

> It is the glory of God to conceal things,
>> but the glory of kings is to search things out. (Prov 25:2)

Do not put yourself forward in the king's presence
    or stand in the place of the great;
for it is better to be told, "Come up here,"
    than to be put lower in the presence of a noble.
(Prov 25:6-7; compare Luke 14:10)

Know well the condition of your flocks,
    and give attention to your herds;
for riches do not last forever,
    nor a crown for all generations. (Prov 27:23-24)

By justice a king gives stability to the land,
    but one who makes heavy exactions ruins it. (Prov 29:4)

It is not for kings, O Lemuel,
    it is not for kings to drink wine,
    or for rulers to desire strong drink;
or else they will drink and forget what has been decreed,
    and will pervert the rights of all the afflicted . . .
Speak out for those who cannot speak,
    for the rights of all the destitute.
Speak out, judge righteously,
    defend the rights of the poor and needy. (Prov 31:4-5, 8-9)

Excavations of Egyptian archives have resulted in texts demonstrating the role of the sage as teacher at the royal court. Two texts in particular are worthy of brief discussion. *The Instruction of Merikare* from the time of the Middle Kingdom (c. 2150 BCE) purports to be advice from the aged reigning king to his son. Not surprisingly, we find the same sort of counsel as found in Proverbs. The king advises his son to be a 'craftsman' in speech, to demonstrate patience with all, to execute justice impartially, and to protect the territorial borders. More directly applicable to our discussion of the sage as teacher in the royal court is *The Instruction of the Vizier Ptah-hotep* from the Old Kingdom (c. 2450 BCE). As the chief advisor to the king, the aging official provides wise counsel to his son, whom he hopes will become the next sage for the monarch. Instructions include eating whatever is served without complaint, laughing when the king laughs, giving rapt attention to all petitioners, and being loyal to friends and wife.

Parent–Child

In addition to the obvious markers of the collection of wise sayings in the book of Proverbs as royal advice, we also note the frequent use of parent-child language. Reflecting the earliest tradition of sage as wise leader of the extended family, the sage offers wisdom from life experiences to educate the family's younger generations. Rather than a royal school for training princes, the family sages offer a "school of hard knocks" for productive subjects. A few examples will illustrate the point.

> Hear, my child, your father's instruction,
>> and do not reject your mother's teaching;
> for they are a fair garland for your head,
>> and pendants for your neck. (Prov 1:8–9)

> My child, do not forget my teaching,
>> but let your heart keep my commandments;
> for length of days and years of life
>> and abundant welfare they will give you. (Prov 3:1–2)

> My child, keep my words
>> and store up my commandments with you;
> keep my commandments and live,
>> keep my teachings as the apple of your eye;
> bind them on your fingers,
>> write them on the tablet of your heart.
> Say to wisdom, "You are my sister,"
>> and call insight your intimate friend,

that they may keep you from the loose woman,
  from the adulteress with her smooth words. (Prov 7:1–5)

Hear, my child, and be wise,
  and direct your mind in the way.
Do not be among winebibbers,
  or among gluttonous eaters of meat;
for the drunkard and the glutton will come to poverty,
  and drowsiness will clothe them with rags. (Prov 23:19–21)

My child, give me your heart,
  and let your eyes observe my ways.
For a prostitute is a deep pit;
  an adulteress is a narrow well. (Prov 23:26–27)

Sage Advice as Wisdom Literature

Today, wise sayings in the Old Testament have become democratized in the sense that readers throughout the generations have recognized their value in building moral character for all people. Scholars recognize "Wisdom Literature" as a genre in the Old Testament that seeks to reflect on the experiences of lived reality and draw conclusions from those experiences that can instruct others. "Wisdom" is the ability to succeed in life by understanding the way the world works and by having the appropriate tools to be able to navigate the culture. Wisdom is to be taught, sought after, meditated on, and followed, in order to have a fulfilling life.

Proverbs

The book of Proverbs espouses character traits that lead to long life and prosperity, especially the five listed below, each of which is illustrated by two proverbs.

Discipline. "Like vinegar to the teeth, and smoke to the eyes, so are the lazy to their employers" (Prov 10:26); "Laziness brings on deep sleep; an idle person will suffer hunger" (Prov 19:15).

Honesty. "A gossip goes about telling secrets, but one who is trustworthy in spirit keeps a confidence" (Prov 11:13); "Bread gained by deceit is sweet, but afterward the mouth will be full of gravel" (Prov 20:17).

Generosity and forgiveness. "Those who are generous are blessed, for they share their bread with the poor" (Prov 22:9); "One who forgives an affront fosters friendship, but one who dwells on disputes will alienate a friend" (Prov 17:9).

Control of anger. "The beginning of strife is like letting out water; so stop before the quarrel breaks out" (Prov 17:14); "Make no friends with those given to anger, and do not associate with hotheads, or you may learn their ways and entangle yourself in a snare" (Prov 22:24).

Moderation in all things. "If you have found honey, eat only enough for you, or else, having too much, you will vomit it" (Prov 25:16); "Like a city breached, without walls, is one who lacks self-control" (Prov 25:28).

Scholars have long noted the remarkable similarities between the Egyptian *Instruction of Amen-em-Opet* and the book of Proverbs, especially the section 22:17—24:22. We do not need to posit necessarily a direct literary link from one to the other. Rather, the coincidence of wise advice evidences the congruence of tradition on how to live successfully as a productive subject in society. We should not be surprised that two different societies would promote the benefits of diligence, honesty, generosity and forgiveness, control of anger, and moderation in all things.

Job

The book of Job is classified as Wisdom Literature, not because it contains pithy sayings like the book of Proverbs, but because it brings life's wisdom to bear on a confounding situation. The righteous main character finds himself inexplicably suffering immensely, mourning the death of his seven sons and three daughters (the perfect family), the destruction of his many livestock and servants, and—perhaps most devastating—the loss of his esteem in the community. His three friends try to convince Job that he must have done something to deserve this terrible plight, because conventional wisdom is that the righteous are rewarded and the wicked are punished. But Job's lived experience points to a different wisdom: it ain't necessarily so. Sometimes the righteous encounter disaster and sometimes the wicked prosper. The book of Job wrestles theologically with making sense of the lived reality of undeserved suffering. This too is wisdom, a lived experience necessary to be able to navigate the vicissitudes of life successfully.

Ecclesiastes

Another wisdom book, Ecclesiastes, approaches the same issue, but with different results. Attributed in the superscription of the book to Solomon, again because of the legendary tradition of Solomon's wisdom, the book is a combination of prose and poetry. The poetic sections are reminiscent of the book of Proverbs. The prose sections narrate the struggle to make sense of lived reality in which death is the great equalizer. "For there is no enduring remembrance of the wise or of fools, seeing that in the days to come all will have been long forgotten. How can the wise die just like fools?" (Eccl 2:16); "For the fate of humans and the fate of animals is the same; as one dies, so dies the other. They all have the same breath, and humans have no advantage over the animals; for all is vanity [ephemeral or transitory]" (Eccl 3:19). The author is struggling with the futility of seeking after wisdom and living as a righteous person, following all the rules, if all persons—wise and righteous as well as foolish and wicked—are confronted with death no matter what.

Some have read the book as an example of pessimistic fatalism: since death comes to all in the end, "eat, drink and be merry" since nothing in life really matters. But the book can also be read as a statement of simple trust in God's provision of a good and decent life to be enjoyed in the present without concern for the inevitable end caused by death. So, for example,

> Go, eat your bread with enjoyment, and drink your wine with a merry heart; for God has long ago approved what you do. Let your garments always be white; do not let oil be lacking on your head. Enjoy life with the wife whom you love, all the days of your vain life that are given you under the sun, because that is your portion in life and in your toil at which you toil under the sun. Whatever your hand finds to do, do with your might; for there is no work or thought or knowledge or wisdom in Sheol [the place of the dead], to which you are going. (Eccl 9:7–10)

Here, the wise sage advises to "eat, drink, and be merry" not because nothing in life matters, but because God is present in all activities of life. Similar advice is found in *The Song of the Harper*, an Egyptian poem from approximately 1300 BCE. Several versions of the poem exist, as apparently entertaining guests at a banquet with harp-playing and songs offering advice was quite popular. Numerous tomb paintings depict such a scene. The song invites guests to enjoy the riches of the banquet, both food and drink without concern, since death comes to all, whether they are satiated or not.

Psalms

Several psalms are categorized as Wisdom literature, since they provide instruction on succeeding in life by acting wisely. Three in particular seem to echo the characterization of wisdom we have discussed in Proverbs, Job, and Ecclesiastes. Psalm 37 is an acrostic poem, meaning that the verses begin with successive letters of the Hebrew alphabet. In the case of this psalm, two verses are used for each letter. So, vv. 1 and 2 begin with an *aleph*, the first letter of the Hebrew alphabet, vv. 3 and 4 begin with *bet*, the second letter, and so forth. (Four letters only have one verse associated with them.) The form of the acrostic poem may lend itself to stringing together independent wise aphorisms. For example,

> Refrain from anger, and forsake wrath.
> Do not fret—it leads only to evil." (Ps 37:8)

> The wicked borrow, and do not pay back,
> but the righteous are generous and keep giving." (Ps 37:21)

These sayings would have been right at home in the book of Proverbs.

Psalm 73 sounds some of the same notes of confusion that are in the book of Job. The psalmist wonders why the wicked flourish and the righteous suffer when conventional wisdom teaches exactly the opposite. For example,

> Such are the wicked; always at ease,
> they increase in riches.
> All in vain I have kept my heart clean
> and washed my hands in innocence.
> For all day long I have been plagued,
> and am punished every morning." (Ps 73:12–14)

The psalmist's resolution is very similar to that of the book of Job:

> I was stupid and ignorant;
> I was like a brute beast toward you.
> Nevertheless I am continually with you;
> you hold my right hand . . .
> My flesh and my heart may fail,
> but God is the strength of my heart and my portion
> forever. (Ps 73:22–23, 26)

The sentiments of Ecclesiastes echo in Psalm 49, as the psalmist muses on the transitory nature of life for both wise and foolish alike. For example,

> "When we look at the wise, they die;
>> fool and dolt perish together and leave their wealth to others.
>
> Their graves are their homes forever,
>> their dwelling places to all generations,
>> though they named lands their own.
>
> Mortals cannot abide in their pomp;
>> they are like the animals that perish." (Ps 49:10–12)

Yet, the psalmist also affirms, "Hear this, all you peoples; give ear, all inhabitants of the world, both low and high, rich and poor together. My mouth shall speak wisdom; the meditation of my heart shall be understanding . . . But God will ransom my soul from the power of Sheol, for he will receive me" (Ps 49:1–3, 15).

The sage, like the king, the prophet, and the priest, longs for a lasting relationship with God. The king is God's earthly representative for enacting justice throughout society, a mirror of the Divine Creator. The prophet announces God's word of judgment and salvation, calling the people into a loyal covenant relationship with their redeemer. The priest accesses the divine presence in the cultus, the prescribed worship rituals designed to repair broken relationships. The sage observes lived reality, exhorting the people of family and kingdom to form a moral character based on the best practices of life with God. All four leadership roles in the Old Testament reflect the character of God, as one who is gracious and merciful, slow to anger, and abounding in steadfast love and faithfulness.

For Further Reading

READERS ARE URGED TO consult biblical commentaries and Bible dictionaries to explore citations and topics.

General Resources

Blenkinsopp, Joseph. *Sage, Priest, Prophet: Religious and Intellectual Leadership in Ancient Israel*. Library of Ancient Israel. Louisville: Westminster John Knox, 1995.

Clements, R. E. *The World of Ancient Israel: Sociological, Anthropological and Political Perspectives*. Cambridge: Cambridge University Press, 1989.

Stevens, Marty E. *Theological Themes of the Old Testament: Creation, Covenant, Cultus, and Character*. Eugene: Cascade Books, 2010.

Vaux, Roland de. *Ancient Israel: Its Life and Institutions*. Translated by R. McHugh. New York: McGraw-Hill, 1961.

Chapter 1: King

Brueggemann, Walter. *David and His Theologian: Literary, Social, and Theological Investigations of the Early Monarchy*. Edited by K. C. Hanson. Eugene: Cascade Books, 2011.

Eaton, John H. *Kingship and the Psalms*. 2nd ed. Biblical Seminar 3. Sheffield: JSOT Press, 1986.

Gnuse, Robert Karl. *No Tolerance for Tyrants: The Biblical Assault on Kings and Kingship*. Collegeville, MN: Liturgical, 2011.

Mowinckel, Sigmund. *He that Cometh: The Messiah Concept in the Old Testament and Later Judaism*. Translated by G. W. Anderson 1954. Reprinted, Grand Rapids: Eerdmans, 2005.

Chapter 2: Prophet

Birch, Bruce C. *Let Justice Roll Down: The Old Testament, Ethics, and Christian Life*. Louisville: Westminster John Knox, 1991.

Petersen, David L. *The Prophetic Literature: An Introduction*. Louisville: Westminster John Knox, 2002.

Stevens, Marty E. "The Obedience of Trust: Recovering the Law as Gift." In *The Ten Commandments: The Reciprocity of Faithfulness*, edited by William P. Brown, 133–45. Library of Theological Ethics. Louisville: Westminster John Knox, 2000.

Weinfeld, Moshe. *Social Justice in Ancient Israel and in the Ancient Near East*. Minneapolis: Fortress, 1995.

Chapter 3: Priest

Cross, Frank Moore. "The Priestly Houses of Early Israel." In *Canaanite Myth and Hebrew Epic: Essays in the History of the Religion of Israel*. Cambridge, MA: Harvard University Press, 1973.

Miller, Patrick D. Jr. *The Religion of Ancient Israel*. Library of Ancient Israel. Louisville: Westminster John Knox, 2000.

Nelson, Richard D. *Raising Up a Faithful Priest: Community and Priesthood in Biblical Theology*. Louisville: Westminster John Knox, 1993.

Stevens, Marty E. *Temples, Tithes, and Taxes: The Temple and the Economic Life of Ancient Israel*. Peabody, MA: Hendrickson, 2006.

Chapter 4: Sage

Clifford, Richard J. *The Wisdom Literature*. Interpreting Biblical Texts. Nashville: Abingdon, 1998.

Gammie, John G., and Leo G. Perdue, editors. *The Sage in Israel and the Ancient Near East*. Winona Lake, IN: Eisenbrauns, 1990.

Murphy, Roland E. *The Tree of Life: An Exploration of the Biblical Wisdom Literature*. Anchor Bible Reference Library. New York: Doubleday, 1990.

Perdue, Leo G. *The Sword and the Stylus: An Introduction to Wisdom in the Age of Empires*. Grand Rapids: Eerdmans, 2008.

Scripture Index

Lightning Source UK Ltd.
Milton Keynes UK
UKOW02f1811030616

275567UK00005B/186/P